NIGHT TRAIN AT WISCASSET STATION

By Lew Dietz

Night Train at Wiscasset Station
A Seal Called Andre (with Harry Goodridge)
The Year of the Big Cat
Touch of Wildness: A Maine Woods Journal
The Allagash

NIGHT TRAIN AT WISCASSET STATION

by Lew Dietz

Photographs by Kosti Ruohomaa

Foreword by Andrew Wyeth
Afterword by Howard Chapnick

Doubleday & Company, Inc.
Garden City, New York
1977

Some of the material in this book has appeared in somewhat different form in *Yankee* magazine and *Down East* magazine.

The interviews with Vital Ouellette and Bert McBurnie in "Tall Timber, Wild Rivers, the Secret Places" were conducted by Lynn Franklin and have been condensed. They were originally published in the *Maine Sunday Telegram*.

Photographs on p. 10 © 1950 Time Inc.; p. 17 © 1971 Howard Chapnick; pp. 20-23 © 1948 Time Inc.; p. 35 © 1945 Time Inc.; pp. 53, 148, 149, 152 © 1959 National Geographic Society; p. 65 © 1951 Time Inc.; pp. 18, 19, 24, 25, 36, 39, 42, 54, 55, 56, 61, 62, 64, 68, 70, 72, 73, 80, 102, 115, 118, 119, 120, 122, 145, 146, 147, 153, 154, 155 © 1977 Black Star Publishing Co., Inc. All photographs have been reprinted by permission of Black Star Publishing Co., Inc.

Designed by Robert S. Nemser

To Kosti Ruohomaa (1914–1961)

Our thanks to Yukiko Launois for the many contributions to the picture selection and the co-ordination of the Ruohomaa negative file.

To Morgan Press whose heritage of printing craftsmanship has been lavished on the faithful reproduction of Kosti Ruohomaa's photographs.

And to photographer Dan McCoy, whose countless hours in the darkroom provided the prints that do full justice to the diverse moods and quality inherent in the photographs of Kosti Ruohomaa.

CONTENTS

Foreword by Andrew Wyeth   9

Kosti Ruohomaa   11

The Character of Maine   27

Maine Is the Land   43

Maine Is the Village   81

The Sea, the Ships, the Running Tides   125

Tall Timber, Wild Rivers, the Secret Places   157

Through a Glass Darkly   185

Afterword by Howard Chapnick   191

Andrew Wyeth in earlier years in the kitchen of the Olsen house with Christina of "Christina's World." Alfaro Olsen, Christina's brother, stands in the background.

Foreword

By Andrew Wyeth

It was on a June evening in 1950 that Kosti Ruohomaa first knocked at my door. I had difficulty pronouncing his name.

"It's like row-home-a-boat," he told me.

That was the beginning of what was for me a warm and rewarding friendship. I had seen his work in the pages of *Life* magazine. They had moved me. His photographs had a mysterious sense of withdrawn reality. It was as if he had been present at some intimate moment and had caught its meaning at the instant of revelation.

Those were the days of trick-angle shots. Kosti avoided trickery. His photographs were candid, but his moments of illumination were caught without the aid of showy dramatic effects. They were the simple truth.

I kept returning again and again to his work. His honest photography possessed the disarming simplicity of a child's nursery rhyme. As in a good painting, one is forever finding something new and fresh and true.

Yes, I will be forever grateful for Kosti Row-Home-a-Boat.

Kosti's Finnish heritage played an enormous part in his genius. Northern people like the Finns, withdrawn though they may appear, are capable of extreme passion. Kosti Ruohomaa had the insight and intelligence to see through his lens the essential character of Maine and its people. He has passed on to all of us a record of his special vision.

A book such as this one which brings together the finest Maine work of this remarkable photographer and celebrates his genius has been long overdue. It is a book to be cherished not only by the people of Maine, but by Americans everywhere.

KOSTI RUOHOMAA

Writing about a departed friend is never an easy assignment. When the good friend, by virtue of his special genius, belongs in the public domain, the task becomes a responsibility. I expect I knew Kosti Ruohomaa as well as it was possible to know that uncommon, problem-racked man. He was scrupulously honest about himself. He deserves nothing but honesty from me.

I knew Kosti for roughly twenty years. I came to know him well just after the war. He was a tall, lithe and handsome young man, gunning cap cocked on his head, camera slung from his neck. I was with him a few days before he died in 1961 at forty-seven. He was a shattered man, bedridden, paralyzed. He was propped up before a box filled with broken glass. With effort he was able to articulate one hand and arm. He managed to operate his camera as he sought abstract beauty in the light refractions of the shards beside his bed.

Within that span of years, Kosti Ruohomaa created his special image of Maine. He said in photographs what he wanted to say, what he had to say. I know of no one who caught Maine more truthfully.

The facts of his life are simple enough. He was born of Finnish parents at Quincy, Massachusetts. An only child, he was brought to Rockland, Maine, as a small boy. He attended the one-room schoolhouse in Rockport, walking the three miles, winter, spring and fall. He graduated from Rockland High School and, despite his father's objections, went to Boston to study art. He worked several years in Boston and New York as a commercial artist, then went to California to work for the Walt Disney Studios as an animator. It was during this period that he took up photography as a hobby. He was never to put his camera down again.

An artist is no more than one with heightened sensibilities and the skills with which to express his insights and communicate his special vision. In the camera, young Ruohomaa found what was for him the perfect tool to express his love of the land, his feeling for Maine and its people.

Under the aegis of the Black Star agency he worked for *Life* and other national magazines for two decades. His base was a small camp on his father's farm on Dodge Mountain, which had been the original family homestead. He never strayed far, or for long, from that eyrie overlooking the sea and backed up to his father's blueberry lands. He made several unsuccessful attempts to tear himself away and find new roots. Perhaps his mind told him that a boyhood home is no more than a womb and that a man can never go home again. The need of his heart overruled his mind.

Kosti Ruohomaa was a working photo-journalist. His work was a job. But despite the discipline that deadlines and assignments forced upon him, the artist prevailed. He photographed what he liked and the way he saw it. He possessed what Cartier-Bresson called ''the eye within.'' The response to his work is the reaction not so much to what he saw but what he felt.

His more telling photographs reveal a love, a pain of parting with a way of life that he saw slipping away. He was a self-appointed archivist of that transitory world caught between the past and the crowding future. Consider his dusk shot of a train at the Wiscasset station. It suggests so much more than the outer reality of a train in a station. We sense that he knew that this would be all but the last train, the end of an era.

When I first knew Kosti he was working for *Life* magazine on a photo essay on a one-room schoolhouse. He chose the little school he'd attended. As a child he'd walked those several miles day after day. He followed another small boy along that course from schoolyard to home. The trap was baited for sentimentalism. The documentation that emerged never departed from tenderness. The total impact upon the viewer was the pure and authentic emotion of an almost unbearable nostalgia.

In his documentation of the Maine scene he never made a banal record: the artist in him refused to settle for the cliché. One summer he had an assignment to do a picture essay on Eastport, Maine, the most easterly town in America. His key shot (similar to the one on page 24) showed a pair of fishermen's long johns blowing on a line straight out in the east wind. As I recall, some irate citizens of that town were incensed at this treatment. They wrote to a state newspaper accusing the photographer of malice.

Malice was not in him. He captured Maine as he saw it, as he felt it. For him, a photograph was not merely a picture of a thing, but a thing in itself. In that study of long johns in the wind he was working with light and space, the compositional elements of tone, line, mass and texture. His concern was to express both the image seen and his emotional response to it and create not a facsimile of nature but a fresh photographic reality.

Kosti Ruohomaa was not the greatest technician. His tools were simple. His basic equipment was a Rolleiflex and a 35mm camera. He worked with color, and toward the end of his life he was beginning to master this new dimension. But he was always more at ease with black and white. Black and white he could control; color seemed to intrude upon his intent, to defeat rather than lend itself to his purpose. Who is to say he was not right? How could color have strengthened the telling picture of his father, body bent over, fighting his way out to the barn in a blinding snowstorm? And what was the need for color in his studies of Maine fog or a Maine landscape on a wintry day?

Kosti was by nature a gregarious man. He loved and needed friends around him. He was an alcoholic and he knew it. I suspect one reason he could not remain long in exile from Maine was this need to be surrounded by old friends who took him the way he was.

Understandably, he was most at ease with creative people. He often dropped in at the studio of my painter wife, Denny Winters, and owned several of her paintings. On his calling list were the Wyeths, Andy and Betsy, Bill and Helen Thon, sculptors George Curtis and Mike Nevelson. The home of Jim Moore, then writer-photographer for the Portland *Press Herald* and his wife Cecile, was one of his favorite ports of call. Sometimes he would arrive with a cookbook and read off mouth-watering recipes until the mistress of the house succumbed and repaired to the kitchen. Peg Shea, an editor of *Down East* magazine, was a familiar. He had little sense of time, and once he called Peg at 3 A.M. for a passage from a Dylan Thomas poem that had eluded him.

After a long day in his darkroom, loneliness would drive Kosti down from the hills like a hunting cat. If he found a friend out, his habit was to leave his calling card, a burned-out flashbulb or an empty beer can. One day, not finding the Andy Wyeths at home, he carved on the dooryard pumpkin, ''Kosti was here.''

He could be a hospitable host when friends conquered the steep, winding road to his hideaway. Friday night in the fall of the year was his special evening to be at home. That was the sauna night, the night he traditionally fired up the rocks in the family Finnish bath. He would have a cookout, usually. Then the entire company would take to the steamhouse—the men first, in Finnish fashion, the ladies when the men were through.

As I recall, only Kosti was inured to take the heat and live steam of the top step in the bath. And from that lofty throne he would expound on art and life in general. He was liberal, politically. He was an incorrigible writer-to-the-editor. He was quite articulate and frequently expressed himself with trenchant wit.

During the final ten years of his life I went on many working trips with Kosti. Together, we covered the Grand Banks in a trawler, the Big Woods on a log drive, the length and breadth of the Canadian Maritimes. We did a Small Town Christmas together, a text-photograph story that appeared in *Collier's* magazine. I would be untruthful if I said he was not at times a problem. But if his drinking excesses were sometimes a strain, the remorse that followed was even harder on his friends.

To say that Kosti Ruohomaa was a tragic figure would be neither fair nor accurate. When he was working at his craft I'm sure he experienced that special joy that only creative people are privileged to know. Years after his death, people would tell me of their meetings with Kosti. One woman told me of seeing this stranger wandering about in the fog on a chill, raw afternoon. He wore only a thin shirt and light pants shoved into a pair of short boots. He was batting about at the edge of the sea, two cameras slung over his shoulder.

She didn't know quite what he was up to, but she asked him in for a cup of coffee. He was shivering and wet to the skin, but he didn't seem aware of it. ''I'm looking at the fog,'' he told her. He didn't offer his name, nor did he ask hers. He drank his coffee quickly and went back to the fog.

There hangs in my study a large blowup Kosti gave me when he lived briefly in our garage apartment. It was, he said, whimsically perhaps, his favorite photograph. It was one of a series he did for *Life*, illustrating old Yankee sayings. This one interpreted "Independent as a Hog on Ice." To tell the truth, I wasn't aware until I saw that photograph that "independent" was something a hog was not. It had taken him several days, with the help of a co-operative farmer, to get that big sow out onto the ice and prove his point. What one sees is utter helplessness: a great fat sow looking straight into the camera's eye with mean, bitter little eyes as if to say, "If this is your idea of a joke, drop dead."

His humor was apt to be of the black variety and frequently turned in upon himself. He sent my wife and me a photograph to serve as his New Year greeting the year before he died. It showed night rain distorting a windowpane, and silhouetted on the sill were two empty bottles. On the back he had scribbled, "Good Togetherness as '60 dawns."

And there was the day we saw the Big Cat. The eastern mountain lion has been listed as extinct in Maine for seventy years. The hardheaded refuse to be convinced that a few members of this feline species still roam our wilderness. They are inclined to dismiss big-cat-sighters as village idiots or, at best, town drunks. Kosti and I were returning from a bass-fishing story, traveling a lonely road in the summer dusk. We saw the shape in the road at the same instant.

"What's that?" Kosti whispered.

I said, "Cut your motor and coast."

We rolled up to within thirty yards of the great beast before he arched off into the deep woods. It was all over in a matter of a few seconds, but that was time enough to see the conformation of his body, the great tail. We stopped and got out of the car. I found one print in the dust of the road. It measured almost five inches across.

"That," I said to Kosti, "was an extinct mountain lion." Back in the car, Kosti began to laugh uproariously. "It's the company you keep. I won't say anything about it, if you don't."

Two years before his death, he had his friend Jim Moore take his portrait, which he dispatched to the obituary file of the Portland *Press Herald*. He wrote: "I knew this was coming sooner or later. Thank heavens none of the flower-throwers are weeping. But why are they laughing?"

It was this dark laughter that cleansed him of any taint of self-pity. He lived on the razor's edge; only his art served to maintain his equilibrium. He trained his camera on the moods of nature and the simple way of Maine life, a life he loved but could never fully share.

We thought pretty much alike about the State of Maine, Kosti and I. Over the years we worked well together in a writer-photographer relationship. As I see it now, I wrote the words, Kosti the music. The intent of this book is to continue this partnership and in the process present an honest portrait of this special region, a pentimento of Maine in transition.

Kosti's base was a small camp on his father's farm. His father's barn loomed large in his view and in his work. Perhaps his mind told him that a man can never go home again . . .

. . . but he seemed to need to preserve the lights and shadows of that special land. . . .

He called upon the memories of his own childhood. His camera once followed a small boy on his laggard way home from a one-room school . . . the route he himself had taken as a boy. . . .

. . . The boy is grown now, the one-room school has vanished.

His work reveals the love, the pain of parting with a way of life he saw was slipping away.

His last New Year's card in 1960 was entitled "Togetherness." His humor was of the black variety and turned in upon himself.

THE CHARACTER OF MAINE

Maine is America's outpost. Look at the map and what one sees is a jut of geography, a handle attached to the corpus of the United States, or, if you will, an appendage. Maine is the only state in the Union with but one sister state for a neighbor. Maine is ringed by woods, mountains and the deep blue sea. This border region has been pretty much on its own from the beginning.

Technically, Maine joined the Union when she shook off the Commonwealth of Massachusetts in 1820. She gained her statehood and at the same time her independence. Maine has remained stubbornly independent ever since.

Maine people like what they are and where they are. Unlike the restless one third of America which moves at least once a year, Maine people are inclined to stay put. Like house cats, they have a strong sense of place. Only the English language has a word for home in the way Maine people think of it: a place where the heart resides.

Clearly, Maine is "different." And just as clearly, Maine moves outside the mainstream of contemporary American life. Countless books have been written describing Maine and her people. To describe and document is not to define. How, then, does one go about anatomizing the character of a region as large and diverse as this most northerly state?

An anthropological investigation might prove enlightening, but it's unlikely that even Margaret Mead in all her wisdom could come up with satisfying conclusions. Maine isn't sufficiently homogeneous to serve as an ethnographic study. Maine has been bombarded by ethnic and cultural influences for centuries.

Emily Dickinson wrote: "I think New Englandly." Is Maine a way of thinking? Yes, and maybe no. Maine people are likely to agree that Maine is the only fit place on earth in which to live and die. On just about any other subject they are disposed to disagree. How else explain the fact that lobstermen co-ops seldom last a year, and town meetings may go on all day and into the night?

Asking a State-of-Mainer what he's all about won't get you very far. Maine Yankees are often accused of answering a question with a question. Is this a form of genial obfuscation or does it betray a disposition to caution, a basic reluctance to be committed? Possibly it's a bit of each. Any reasonable man will see two sides to any given question. The Maine Yankee, operating efficiently, will see a good half dozen. His rhetorical repertoire includes "yes and no," "most generally," "maybe so" and a laconic "depends." Nor can you get a Maine painter or carpenter to come right out and say, "I'll be there Monday." He much prefers, "Along about Monday." A dyed-in-the-wool State-of-Mainer simply refuses to be pinned down.

Can it be argued that there exists a genus *Homo sapiens mainiacus*? Webster defines "species" as a group of individuals or objects having certain distinguishing characteristics. And biologists tell us that a new species is sometimes created when genetic flow is blocked by geographic barriers which isolate a mutant from the parent stock.

In the case of Maine this thesis is not entirely persuasive. Maine indeed is isolated; but coastal Maine, where 80 per cent of the population was—and still is—concentrated, has from the beginning enjoyed open seaward communication, not only within the region but with the whole eastern seaboard as well. Indeed, far from being victims of a provincial society, Maine seamen in the Homeric age of sail were citizens of the world.

In the face of the evidence, it must be accepted that whatever it is that Maine has, it's mighty potent and durable stuff. If one accepts that basic Maine attitudes have not changed appreciably since pioneer days, then the first step is to attempt to isolate some of the key ingredients which constitute the character of Maine. The bedrock characteristic, it seems to me, is a stubborn independence of thought and action. Call it the frontier syndrome or, if you will, a persistent strain of primitive, old-fashioned Americanism.

Historically, this independent spirit has presented a problem to others. When the Massachusetts Bay Colony took Maine under its wing in 1677, the avowed motive was to do the work of the Lord by civilizing these free-thinking, free-living settlers of the "Eastern Lands." It was a losing battle from the outset. These Maine frontiersmen had come to fish and clear land. They had little use for religious zealots, and even less for the English king and his avaricious agents bent on policing their activities.

This trait we call pride has a wide range of meanings. Maine's pride comes in several varieties. Maine people demonstrate a quiet self-esteem, but are prone as well to overreact in defense of their native heath. The statehood Maine gained in 1820 brought forth an orgy of self-exaltation. To this day, native sons think of themselves not only as being from Maine, but from the *State* of Maine, by God!

Maine didn't get along much better with her neighbors to the north. In the early 1840s Maine lumbermen all but got us into a shooting war with Canada over real and imagined transgressions. One may be sure that the cooler heads that prevailed were not on the necks of Maine men.

This prickly pride is exposed in a number of curious ways. It's all very well to refer to a Maine-born man as a native son, but the bald term "native," particularly when it's employed by summer people, is something else again. In the Mainer's view, there is something pukka sahib about the word, suggesting the primitive peoples of the emerging nations.

Nor will Maine women work for summer folk except on their own terms. In Maine's all but strata-less society there has never existed a servant class. A Maine woman is perfectly willing to accept good money working as a cook or a domestic for a summer family so long as it is clearly understood she is not being hired by her betters, but has come in merely to "help out." Summer people who don't grasp this semantic subtlety usually find themselves doing their own dirty work.

In order to understand such stiff-necked attitudes it's necessary to place the State of Maine in proper historical perspective. During its early history, southwestern Maine was the extension of New England society and the forward line of settlement. It wasn't until well into the eighteenth century that the flow pushed beyond the region of Falmouth (Portland). Much of the wild territory between the Georges River at Thomaston and Canada was a no-man's-land caught between the vying colonial forces of the French and the English.

Maine was and still is a frontier. Maine people continue to be engaged in a battle with nature and an austere environment.

It may well be that a fair share of Maine's people today are engaged in trades, services and industry, but it is from its cadres of fishermen, woodsmen, trappers and farmers that Maine attitudes continue to be nurtured. It was the predisposition to resent all privileges based on wealth and class which colored Maine frontier attitudes. And this prejudice persists to this day.

Little wonder that the patricians of New England's landed society found these Maine settlers "common, coarse, practical, sturdy and independent." John Josselyn, a seventeenth-century investigator, could find very little he liked about Maine yeomen. He reported that most of the Maine farmers "have the custom of taking tobacco, sleeping at noon, sitting long at meals sometimes four times a day, and now and then drinking a dram of a bottle extrao[r]dinarily."

Maine, of course, has its promoters and Chamber of Commerce drum-beaters, but at the grassroots level Maine people tend to be grateful that Maine doesn't please everybody. Maine people are quite aware of what they have and, wrongheaded though they may appear to be in some instances, they are inclined to resist any effort toward abrupt change. Maine citizens are certainly in no hurry to be dragged feet first into the present century.

It is said that State-of-Mainers are downright unfriendly to strangers and johnny-come-lately residents. Certainly Maine villages don't go in for the Welcome Wagon folderol employed in some sectors of American suburbia. On the other hand, one sure way for a stranger to meet his neighbors is to get his car stuck in a snowdrift. Maine people are not so much xenophobic as cautious. Typically, the Maine native will reserve any judgment until newcomers are, as he puts it, "summered and wintered."

Maine people have more reason than ever to be cautious. Maine is faced today with ever-increasing pressures from new waves of settlers: a mixed bag of retirees, young homesteaders, developers, romantics and escapees from postindustrial America. These latter-day settlers tend to agglutinate and form enclaves which exert political and social influence. Maine people complain, with some justification, that it is the people who are attracted to Maine because it is relatively "unspoiled" who proceed to direct their energies to changing Maine in the name of progress.

Certainly Maine has not enjoyed progress in the commonly accepted meaning of the word. While the population of the rest of America has increased seventeen times since 1920, Maine's has just barely doubled. And as another measure of Maine's delay in terms of the Union's growth, Maine started out with eight congressmen and today must be satisfied with two.

There are, of course, good citizens who mutter at Maine's stepchild role in this affluent society and decry the resistance to industrialization with the job opportunities it would bring to Maine. But curiously, there were few outcries when passenger trains stopped running into the state a decade ago. It appears to be the firm conviction of many of the Maine citizenry that since there's no legal way to keep people from coming to Maine, the least that can be done is to make it as inconvenient as possible.

If Maine people are aware of what they have, they are no less aware of who they are. Maine may stand as an anomaly in the rootless and nomadic society that America has become. Maine villages are still largely composed of third- and fourth-generation families. To be born and to remain in the place of one's father and father's father lends the continuity so essential to the feeling of identity.

The closeness of Maine people to the natural world around them has been another stabilizing factor. Not even a Maine city man need travel far to find good hunting and fishing or a natural sanctuary. Those who live their lives in an arena where man is dominated by nature gain the hardihood of spirit to withstand the stresses which can destroy those who are without roots in the earth.

Possibly it is the security that comes of belonging which has nurtured in Maine people a tolerance both moral and intellectual. A tincture of this laissez-faire attitude colors all areas of Maine life. In Maine villages, town drunks and village idiots roam at large along with a full complement of town dogs and an occasional transvestite. All Maine villages have their quotas of gossips, bad-mouthers and bigots, but, along with other sinners, they are accepted as evidence of the imperfectibility of man.

Early Maine settlers deplored the bigotry manifested by the Salem witch hunts. Although wealthy landowners in colonial Maine commonly owned slaves, these blacks were accorded a degree of civil and religious freedom. They were accepted as church members, could hold property and testify in courts of justice. During the antebellum days, Maine was an important link in the Underground Railway. Many an old Maine house boasts a secret room where runaway slaves were hidden en route to Canada and freedom.

This insistence upon the rights of the individual can result in a mild form of anarchy. As noted earlier, Mainers see at least two sides to every question. A town meeting may dispose of a two-hundred-thousand-dollar school budget in ten minutes and then devote hours to the two-hundred-dollar question of whether snow should be machine loaded or hand loaded into trucks. To speak out and be heard is a right dearly cherished. Perhaps only in a Maine town meeting is the one-man, one-vote principle a political reality.

Perhaps most exasperating to those uninitiated into Maine's arcane society is the State-of-Mainer's resistance to legal controls, even when such controls are obviously in the common interest. Maine people will get together voluntarily and work with a will to rebuild the house of the burned-out neighbor, but they don't like to be told what to do. The very word "zoning" is charged, and efforts to pass zoning ordinances can be counted on to arouse emotions. Maine paid not the slightest attention to the Eighteenth Amendment, and so-called "ardent spirits" were sold openly. However, Mainers are strict constitutionalists on the issue of the right to keep and bear arms. A Maine politician proposes gun control only at his peril.

The ever-lurking danger in any attempt to understand the Maine psyche is to be beguiled by stereotypes. Although outlander writers have most frequently erred in this respect, Maine scriveners must share some of the guilt. Certainly, Kenneth Roberts and Robert P. Tristram Coffin did their level best to canonize the native product. But it was the apotheosizing by wide-eyed nineteenth-century visitors which set the style and accomplished the distortion. Wrote James Russell Lowell after a trip to the Maine wilds: "I have never seen a finer race of men . . . they appear to have been hewn out of the northwest passage through wintry snows to those spicelands of character."

Fortunately, there are in the public domain Maine archetypes to balance such embarrassing effusions. There is the sharp trader to match the philosopher-storekeeper; the monosyllabic hayseed to stand off the taciturn lobsterman. And the Maine Yankee may just as easily be viewed as niggardly rather than "careful," or a stubborn mossback rather than a rugged individualist.

As the saying goes, you pays your money and takes your choice; but the truth of the nature of Maine and its people would not be served by gross simplification. It is doubtful if there exists a typical Down East Yankee. Maine people don't accommodate to standardization: they have thus far escaped the grinding wheel of conformity.

In the final analysis, the Maine character has been shaped by the conditions and the imperatives of the harsh habitat in which its people have lived and endured. Maine people are special because the factors which control and govern their lives are special and, to some degree, limiting. The white pine, the state symbol, may disperse a million seeds, yet seedlings sprout only where mineral soil has been exposed.

In short, not anyone can live in Maine or would wish to. Those few who have found Maine soil optimum for their nourishment have remained to become rooted. Like the white pine, the State-of-Mainer is here because he belongs here.

The myth that is Maine is woven inextricably with the truth. The likelihood is that the people of Maine are no more capable of distinguishing the difference than those outlanders who view Maine from afar or who move in and out of this region with the seasons. The image of Maine as a sequestered place caught in a back eddy of the present century, a repository of the American past where farmers still seek weather answers from the sky, where woodsmen are wise and boatbuilders believe in taking pains, where hardy fishermen toil with their nets in fair weather and foul, and mothers make the best blueberry pies on earth—a golden idealization though it may be—is somehow persuasive and even credible to the people of Maine.

It may well be that those who call Maine home help to encourage and perpetuate the myth, for they wish desperately that it be true. To endure, a people must treasure the image of itself. Maine people cling to this image as a precious heritage, and herein may lie the true strength of Maine.

MAINE IS THE LAND

Winter

Responding to a religious question from a Danish Arctic explorer a half century ago, the Eskimo shaman said, "We fear the cold and the things we do not understand."

The snow and cold, the wintry bleakness, long have been the stark bedfellows of northern New Englanders. Since the days of the first settlements, Maine people have thought of the brumal season as "the long hard winter." Perhaps the deep fear primitives knew has eased with understanding, but the respect for winter remains.

Though a heavy fall of soft, wet snow may be called an "old-fashioned snowstorm," it is doubtful if winters have changed for better or worse over the span of recent generations. Our attitude has altered. Roads must be cleared, cars moved and schedules met. Snow is no longer a sometime joy and boon to man: it is an unmitigated nuisance.

Our rural forebears referred to snow as "poor man's fertilizer." The old saying "a snow year is a good year" suggests that our grandfathers counted snow among their blessings. At the least, they were inclined to make the best of something they could do nothing about.

The Old Fellow remembering his Maine boyhood muses, "When it snowed we stayed home, or if we had to go someplace, we walked. The roads were smoothed down for a few teams to get about, but mostly we stayed put. There was always enough to eat in the house and wood to keep us warm. We saw to that."

Though northern New Englanders no longer submit to winter with easy grace, they remain reconciled to snow and ice. They have not relaxed their vigilance. It is as though these winter-seasoned people suspect a cozenage in the proclaimed wonders of the modern age. They are not yet convinced that man has conquered his environment. All too often they are reminded that he has not.

Maine people need only to look about them to see the evidence of the recent Ice Age. Glacier-scarred boulders across the landscape are reminders of the abiding winters from which northern man has emerged. The first task of the settlers was to remove those boulders from the land by bone labor so that they might plow and sow. Through those first Maine winters the process of selection was operative: only those who contended and endured remained to greet the spring. Not yet expunged from the Maine psyche is the feeling that the flowering spring must be earned to be appreciated. To prepare for winter is a ritual too deeply rooted to be lapsed.

Even in the villages the hallowed custom of ranking fir boughs and banking boards around house foundations dies hard. "It's good for the house," the Old Fellow might remark, as though the elderly home calls for indulgence rather than himself. And always there are pipes to protect from freezing, storm windows to install, and supplementary wood stoves to set up in vulnerable nooks.

Backcountrymen are even more reluctant to change old habits. There are woodpiles to be replenished, animals to be kept warm; and yet a few still set cider by to harden and cram root cellars with winter's supply of potatoes, rutabagas, onions and

Hubbard squashes. By the time the field mice slip into the houses and crickets chirr at the hearth, Maine country people are ready, come what may.

Winter is a season that calls for character and stamina. Maine people take a quiet pride in a "real buster of a winter." Perversely perhaps, they take wry pleasure in the spectacle of modern man getting his come-uppance at the hand of nature. The Old Ones are disposed to brag a bit about the snowstorms they experienced in an earlier day, much as though there is honor in having survived them. They speak of the year they were forced to tunnel into the grocery store, and the winter the ice was so thick on Penobscot Bay men could drive teams across the ice to Islesboro.

The northern winter comes quietly like a stalking cat. Unlike spring, which arrives with a sudden burst of life, or autumn which explodes into flame with the first frosts, the Maine winter contemplates its passage; it is a progressive silence which begins with the southbound flights of birds and the final fading of the insect hum. Wind and rain strip the last leaves from the hardwoods; then the first snowfall covers the brown land. And winter is here.

Maine people have always lived in the long shadow of winter. Like the creatures whose northern land they share, they have come to accept the tyranny of this the longest season, which more than all the other seasons governs and restricts their lives.

Winter has a way of bringing man face to face with himself. Winter is a quiet time, the season of nature's rest and man's contemplation. Though the earth pulse is slowed, life persists. The Maine countryman needs only to step from his door into the tucked-in wintry world to see the evidence. Once snow covers the earth, nature is an open book. Everything that moves leaves its record. There are the fresh stitcheries fashioned by squirrels and foraging field mice. The mouse trail vanishes in a clump of grass to emerge again. On the pristine blanket—whiter than the whitest wash—he may see the end of the story. The lacy track ends abruptly where the marks of an owl's wing brush the snow.

Sudden death in the woods is too natural and commonplace to qualify as drama in nature's terms. The Maine rabbit hunter is well aware that the rabbit is not there for him and his hounds, but to assure a food supply for the owls, the bobcats, the foxes and all those other creatures that must struggle to survive the harsh northern winter. There exists in him the awareness that the ultimate object of nature's stewardship is the welfare of the totality of things.

There is a discernible rhythm to the Maine winter. By the time the first snow comes everyone is ready for a breather. For one thing, the last of the "visitors" have left; Maine people have the state to themselves. The time has come to get to know one another again, to pass the time of day. December is a social time. The ladies have their church sales and baked-bean suppers. All over Maine the lights of Christmas come on.

January is the month of cold, the period of subfreezing days and subzero nights. The old houses creak as the chill penetrates the timbers. The January thaw, if it comes at all, is no more than a brief respite of slush and yard-long icicles, glittering swords of Damocles pendant from eaves. February is the month of snow, the heart of winter, the time of deepest stillness. By the time February has run its course, winter for many is like the guest who has outstayed his welcome.

Groundhog Day, February second, has been duly noted, of course. Not that Maine people take much stock in the ancient myth. The chubby marmot, known in Maine as the woodchuck, has too much sense to emerge from his hole to check his shadow at that early date. In any event, no seasoned Mainer would be lulled into accepting an optimistic prophecy.

Not that Maine people are incorrigible pessimists, as some would have it. Lacking the trust that spring having always come will come again, they would have given up long ago. The good word that goes about once the back of February is broken—"it's all downhill to spring"—is a measure of that optimism.

Of course, there is the April mud season to endure, and perhaps one final sneaky snowstorm; but once the news that the ice is out of the back ponds is confirmed, there is no longer any doubt that spring once again has established a beachhead.

And then on that first warm April evening comes the clinching confirmation: the primordial chorus of peepers issues from the bogs. Some of nature's signals may be devious, but this is one sign that has never failed.

Spring comes as a deliverance to northern New England, a victory hard won and therefore to be savored. All too quickly man forgets the tunnel of snow through which he emerged. A Maine winter serves as a reminder.

Maine people would have it no other way. For all their muttering through long, hard winters, they are inclined to pity those Americans who must live in regions where the snow never falls and winter is little more than a browning of the earth.

Spring

If winter is a test of endurance, the Maine spring is a trial of patience. The newcomer may contend that Maine has no spring, but in its stead three months of gray limbo until the summer solstice, when suddenly it is summer.

Admittedly, the northern spring is a long, capricious interlude of fits and starts and false promises, but for those who have lived their lives close to the land, to bear witness to its laggard progress is a privilege not to be forgone. In the past as now, the "mud season" was an abomination. It is nonetheless a bounden promise. Spring comes to Maine while winter still holds sway—not in any substantial form, but manifest in an aura of expectancy palpable to those attuned to the awakening earth.

In the deep woods one may hear the music of running rills and brooks swollen by the melting snow. Fat partridges perch in the alders, stuffing themselves on plump buds. Myriads of dancing snow fleas darken the banks of rotting snow.

Then, after the first warm southerlies, comes the resounding ping of ice settling on the ponds, fair warning to smelt fishermen that the time has come to haul their shacks ashore.

Now, as in the past, spring means different things to different people. For some, it's the first robin; for others, a shy crocus bloom or sap buckets hanging from the boles of rock maples.

Immemorially, spring in Maine was fiddlehead time. Along with pumpkins, sweet corn and maple syrup, the Abnakis initiated the settlers in the delights of fiddlehead greens, those tender young tips of the ostrich fern that push up through the silt in woodland glades after the spring runoff.

The time has passed when fiddleheading was all but an obligatory enactment in the rites of spring and the locations of productive beds were family secrets as jealously held as the recipe for Grandma's mince pie; but appreciators still abound in the Maine countryside. Yet ask a country wife what a fiddlehead tastes like, you'll get a puckered brow. A cross between an artichoke and asparagus perhaps? Broccoli with a touch of mushroom? Then a smile and a shrug. For her, there is nothing else in the world that tastes like a fiddlehead green.

There is no progressive order to the coming of the northern spring: it can be one step forward and two back, a series of soft days and then a sudden backlash of winter in the form of a honking northeast snowstorm. The downright contrariness of a Maine spring lends spice and adventure to its unfolding. April may arrive under leaden skies and spitting snow; yards littered with winter's detritus soggy as old pudding; grimy snow lying in slumping windrows along the highway shoulders.

Yet the walker in the fields will be heartened by signs that winter's days are numbered. His frolicking dog may put up an arriving killdeer, sending it off in jagged flight, sounding its shrill alarm cry as it goes. Farther along he may hear the sweet wistful call of a phoebe: and down along the shore of lake or sea, the raucus chorus of spring crows, the earliest of returning migrants. There are those who insist they can distinguish between the calls of the resident and transient crows: the fresh arrivals are more vociferous than their stay-at-home brothers. It's as if they wish to compensate for their pusillanimity in opting to escape from winter's rigors.

For spring watchers, April brings what is to all but the dullard the most stirring of spring harbingers. The sound comes first to the ear, a plangent honking, distant, then swelling to a wild diapason. Ranging eyes next descry the ragged formation of Canada geese scraping a frieze of naked trees. The flock may veer suddenly and the pitch of the chorus lowers to a deep chuckling, the sound of geese sighting a feeding ground and preparing to light upon some ice-free pond.

So for all the bleak aspect of the landscape, the curtain rises. Once the geese fly in from the South, the gentle hooting of the mourning dove may be heard in the land. The "voice of the turtle" which marked the coming of spring in biblical lands was a sound rarely heard by Yankee grandfathers. Like the mockingbird, this soft-spoken dove is relatively new to Maine and its spring song most welcome to winter-weary northerners.

But Maine spring will not be hurried. April advances, yet the winter birds—blue-jays, evening grosbeaks, purple finches—have the feeders more or less to themselves. A few redwings and robins trickle in—males preparing to stake claims to nesting sites for the most part. They find little to sing about. And more often than not, they pay for their audacity. Along comes a sneak snowstorm to drop a foot of snow upon the land. The emergent spring is stopped in its tracks.

In an earlier day, a snow that fell in April was called a "robin snow." It was said to draw the last frost from the ground and bring the earthworms to the surface. This white incursion is gratefully brief. A high sun and a few days of warm rain make short work of the snow blanket: spring reforms its ranks and continues its ineluctable forward march.

Now woodcock are moving in from their wintering grounds in the Deep South. These shy oddfellows of the damp alder runs, finding some difficulty in drilling for worms in the half-frozen earth, forage in the open glades where sun has softened the earth.

Then upon some soft morning comes the sweet fluting of a solitary white-throated sparrow. Known to our grandfathers as the peabody bird, his spring song putatively exhorts Farmer Peabody to sow wheat, though quite obviously it is too soon to sow anything less hardy than lettuce and peas. The sparrow attempts no more than a few tentative bars before subsiding into an embarrassed silence.

Then, when it appears that spring is mired in the mud somewhere south of Boston, a spell of warm, sunny days blesses the land like a benediction. The ice on the ponds grows porous and darkens to the color of gunmetal. Ice-out occurs without fanfare: one day the pond is locked in ice; the next, open water reflects the sky. In a glimmering, spring casts its last thralls.

Though the magical moment may come as early as mid-April in southern regions of Maine and as late as mid-May in the North Woods, this is the point of no return. Now there can be no turning back. The dalliance is over: Maine spring will come on in a rush to meet its immemorial appointment with summer.

As they have each year in Maine's long memory, the lilacs bloom on Memorial Day. Like the long-distance runner, Maine spring saves its kick for the final lap. And suddenly it is summer.

Summer

For those who live on memories, the Maine summer is crowded with ghosts. The dusty road with its familiar hollows and ruts has turned smooth and black. Creaking wheels and booted walkers no longer pass, traveling from farm to store, to church and school. Other than the blacktop road, the change to the eye is small: the green hills, the curve of the river, the stone walls are still there. The place remains, though the human change is vast.

The Maine farmer, so recently the heart of rural life, is diminished as his hardscrabble acres shrink to garden patches. The hayloft is empty, the horse stalls, the tie-up for cattle, vacant. The field may be mowed, the hay baled, though hay is no longer a cash crop; but the battle must go on to keep the land from returning to wilderness. The Maine countryman loves the fields that his forebears worked dawn to dark, wresting from the wilds. His is a delaying action, an orderly retreat.

A hot summer day finds a lean, weathered man leaning against a single gas pump in front of the crossroads store. If he's of a mind to talk, he'll tell you his farm is up for sale. The boys have left; the girls too. He's put a fancy price on his land, he'll say without much pleasure. Perhaps it is his hidden thought that the price will hold back change, delay the inevitable.

He may not say what he may know full well: that the small dirt farmer will go the way of the Indian; that he is the new vanishing race. What he will say without particular rancor: "It's the taxes. The taxes are wicked." And from long habit he will look at the sky and say, "We need rain bad."

The Maine summer is brief, a mere hyphen connecting spring and autumn. Once it was a time of summer boarders who came by train or on the "Boston Boat" to rusticate for weeks or months and to depart as quietly as they came. Today, Maine is burdened by a summer increment of millions. The initial invasion began before the century's turn when wealthy families from the major cities trekked to Maine to seek the "simple life." Great sprawling "cottages," staffed with servants, took up prime sites along the coast. These enclaves of the privileged superimposed a new way of life upon the old. The members of these summer dynasties had no need or wish to be "accepted"; they wished rather to be served and to establish a vassalage of those whose forebears had known the sort of glory that came from building windships and sailing them to the far corners of the earth.

It was a full half century before coastal Maine freed itself from the baronial burden. Buttressed fortunes did not survive the quiet American social revolution. The new breed, many the sons and daughters of the earlier dynasties, came with more grace and less money and more modestly called themselves "summer residents." They hold in common with the native stock a love of place and a wish to keep the world they borrow for seasonal escape safe from despoliation. Yet an otherness persists: they are welcomed, even indulged, but differences too wide to bridge continue to separate these seasonal migrants from the indigenous stock.

For a century, summer people have been a manageable fact of Maine life. Now a new wave of summer invaders is threatening to change the summer face of Maine. The social revolution that leveled wealth has made possible another and larger class of vacationers. The shibboleth VACATIONLAND is luring to the state a mixed bag of holidayers, trippers, motel-hopping sightseers. In increasing numbers they jam the highways and byways, seeking "quaintness," accepting the meretricious as reality, consuming seafood platters, and buying knicknacks produced for the most part by camp followers who move in for a quick harvest.

Perhaps it is just as well that Maine summer is brief. It is only because the season passes quickly that devastation is held at bay and irreparable damage to the native fabric averted. Cupidity may flourish under summer skies, but the span is too short for deep rooting. The lady who phones from New York to inquire of a cottage owner if the beds are comfortable may still be told, "No ma'am, they ain't." Perhaps the beds are equipped with innerspring mattresses, but to tell the lady that would amount to pandering. The visitor may interpret such behavior as perverse; but it is no more than a reminder that the vacationers come on Maine terms, that no amount of money will buy a touched forelock.

For those who call Maine home, summer has become a season of alloyed pleasure, a time of waiting for its end. With cool August nights, the green fields turn tawny, the dusty roadsides burgeon with goldenrod, wild aster and purple vetch; the blueberry lands are transformed to Persian carpets. As abrupt as a slamming door, Labor Day brings to a close this season of mixed blessings. September's harvest moon serves warning that killing frosts are on their way. By the time of October's hunter's moon, the trauma of summer has been healed, health and sanity restored.

Autumn

For all its festive dress, the northern autumn carries overtones of sadness, a sense of the year drawing in, of all life slowing. By early October, wind and rain have stripped the hardwoods. The flinty mountainside, slashed by a sleet of naked birches, looms closer. Just ahead of the freezing earth, flocked robins flee southward. Strings of honking geese hasten to wintering grounds. Indian summer, that indeterminate spell of bluebird weather, whets the unease: it is a borrowed blessing that must be paid for dearly.

"Once the cold was set, we killed a hog," the Rememberer said. "We'd lived without meat for months and for a spell we splurged. There was a deer hanging usually, maybe two. Mother tagged John's first deer, though she hated guns and didn't like being a party to the deceit. Thanksgiving lasted most of a month. Then the first snow put a damper on that. We commenced to think of the winter ahead. We commenced to think of sharing our plenty and seeking our friends before the snow closed us in. Most of all, we looked forward to the Country Fair. Busy or not, most of us just picked up and went.

"In my grandfather's time most villages of any bigness had their Fair Grounds. There was a dirt track and long barnlike buildings where the ladies showed baked stuff, preserves and patchwork quilts; the men showed hogs and cattle. We didn't need much money, for there was little to buy save a bag of peanuts or a ride on the merry-go-round. There were horse races, horse and cattle pulls and kid scrambles for a calf or a greased pig. We came in the morning bringing our lunches and stayed until dark."

Most of those village Fair Grounds are choked with weeds. The Country Fair has not yet departed from the Maine scene, but some of its rural flavor and informal sociability has been lost by the wayside. Once exclusively an autumn festival, the meets begin now in July to profit from the summer visitors. Along tawdry midways hard-faced strangers bark their wares of rides and raree-shows; the prizes to be won are of little value. Overwhelming the smell of trampled grass are the odors of deep-fry fat and spun-sugar candy. Dust stings the eyes and litter blows in the wind.

It is only when the leaves turn that something of the remembered joy emerges from the gaudy trappings. With cool nights and the last bright days, the Maine Country Fair becomes gay, personal and unmistakably rural. The midways shrink and crowds gather around the cattle pens and drawing pits. And, as it has for a century, the call goes out: "Hustle those cattle in here, you drivers, it's time for the drawing."

The rules for this venerable competition are loose and ever have been. Over the years, each fair has established its own. Be it a pair of oxen or workhorses, a matched team is required to haul a laden sled, or stoneboat, a prescribed distance. Weight is added to the boat after each heat until one pair hauls a load that none of the others can manage.

"Tiny" Macgruder, a hulk of a man, leans against his waiting pair by the drawing pit. "Pshaw," Tiny said with a smile, "I don't do this for the money. Why, what prize money I win wouldn't feed those babies for a week. I take in the fall fairs for the fun. Maybe the last time before the winter funerals to get to meet my friends."

Gray is the color of Maine's November. Gunmetal skies, rain or spitting snow. In the North Country the slush runs have begun on the rivers; the back ponds are caught. There is snow calf-deep in the high country. The snowshoe rabbit is changing his coat from brown to winter-white. The Christmas season comes with December to close out the year. To cut and fetch in the tree is a family affair of long and honored tradition. The fir balsam is the Maine Christmas tree. No other will do.

Will Leonard removed the tattered match from his teeth. "Last Christmas Eve I caught Harry Ames buying a tree for two dollars at the shopping plaza. A boughten Christmas tree! Can you bend that!"

It was a decade before the American Revolution that Isaiah Tolman built his house in the hill back from the coast. Like Christmases past, family history is a tapestry of memories passed down over the centuries. Earl Tolman has recalled a boyhood Christmas when the century was young, printed in part in the local paper.

"My father was a dairy farmer. Christmas or not, there was work to be done. I remember my father coming to the foot of the stairs and calling, 'Time to milk.' I would wake, light the lamp, and look at the clock. Four-thirty. When us boys got down—there were five of us and one girl—the lanterns were all ready for the barn. We had a hundred head of cattle to milk and it took about three hours. When all the cows were milked, cleaned and fed, it would be eight o'clock. And this being Christmas, we didn't have any other chores, save taking care of the cows and horses.

"By the time we got back to the kitchen, mother would have our breakfast of either oatmeal or cornmeal mush. Then she would bring on the hot biscuits along with eggs and bacon. Right after breakfast some of us boys would harness up the driving horse and sleigh and go over to Ingraham Corner and bring back mother's father and mother to have Christmas with us. When we were all together, we had our tree. It wasn't a tree like they have today. There were no lights and few decorations: popcorn and cranberry strings, colored paper, peanuts in the shell, and of course long stockings. The oldest boy would play Santa and hand out the gifts.

"There was very little money, so the gifts were things mother could make, like sweaters, mittens and other things to wear made from homespun yarn. Father would make such things as toy carts for the younger children and skis made of barrel staves for the older boys. When the tree was bare, those with sleds and skis would grab up their presents and make for the hill. The older boys would take up their guns, call the dog and head into the Bog to hunt rabbits. Mother would tell us all to be sure to be home to dinner at one.

"You can be sure that Christmas dinner was something we weren't going to miss. On the table was turkey, roast pork, cranberries from the Bog, sweet potatoes, turnips, and of course homemade bread, Indian pudding, pumpkin and chocolate pies. When we were all seated, Father would say, 'Whoever's turn it is to say grace, please do so.'

"After dinner the men went into the living room and the ladies cleared the table. When the ladies joined the men, all us boys were there too, for it was storytelling time. My grandfather Blake had gone West by wagon train in the Gold Rush and he would tell of his adventures. Later in the afternoon, Mother would make molasses candy for us to pull. Then Father would say, 'Time for chores,' and we'd head for the barn and one of the boys would get the horse and sleigh and take Gramp and Gran home. That was the way it was back when I was a boy. We didn't have what boys have today, but we had a lot. I remember my father saying, 'Son, be honest, be just, and fear not, and you will be as good as any person, even though you are a farmer.' "

Villager or farmer, the place is the cherished nourishment, and the fear is of the winds of change that threaten to alter the shape of the land and offer little of human value in return.

Life in the Maine past was not easy. Maine backcountry life walked the narrow edge of subsistence. Look at their faces in browning albums. Even the young men in full pride of vitality bear marks of long labor in the fields and woods. The old men settled as gnarled figures, the women opulent in middle years, thinned too soon, dried up like garden stalks, hands knotted, joints swollen by years of washing and scrubbing.

Yet, real or illusory, the past holds a fragrance of a good life, satisfying and secure. It was a time when it was reward enough for a man to be buried under the soil he had plowed. The feeling is that there is something wrong in asking too much. It isn't that life is changing, but that it is changing too fast.

Underlying the uneasiness is the fear of disinheritance. This fear of losing the land is not shouted aloud, but whispered as a prayer. In quietness lies the hope that the rushing world may pass them by.

The northern winter comes quietly . . .

. . . like a stalking cat . . .

. . . . *a season of contemplation.*

Wind and rain strip the hardwoods . . .

. . . the first snow covers a brown land.

Maine people have come to accept winter's tyranny . . .

64

. . . they are inclined to pity those who live where snow never falls.

Maine spring is a capricious season of fits and starts and false promises. For those who live close to the soil, to bear witness to spring's uncertain progress is a privilege not to be forgone.

*The Maine summer is crowded with ghosts. Creaking wheels and booted walkers
no longer pass along the dusty road . . .*

. . . yet the green hills, the flowering pastures, the stone walls are still there. Though the human change is vast, the place remains.

The northern autumn has overtones of sadness, the sense of the year drawing in, all life slowing.

76

With the cool nights and the last bright days, the Maine Country Fair becomes gay, personal and unmistakably rural, with horse and cattle-pulling contests, midways and harness races. Says a cattle handler at the drawing pits, "May be the last time before the winter funerals to meet my friends."

MAINE IS THE VILLAGE

Maine Pentimento

Back in the early fifties a journalist came to Maine to do a story on one of the state's rising political figures. Hoping to find some clues to the character of his subject, he poked around the farms and villages of rural Maine. As he prepared to depart he was asked what of significance he had learned about the state.

"I learned one thing," the journalist replied, "Maine people don't throw anything away."

The comment was made in jest, but the fact that Maine people hold on to things should not be underestimated as a vital clue to the nature of the Maine Yankee. Nor can this residual trait of reusing and making do be dismissed as a Puritan hangover of equating waste with sin. The full answer lies deeper. Like a twice-told tale, an old kettle or a well-worn hat is a part of the past, an artifactual reminder: it is imbued with the stuff of history.

In a like context it has been said that the dearth of hard money and a plethora of stony soil nourished Yankee ingenuity: it required resourcefulness merely to survive. There is truth there, but again the contriving out of bits and pieces, the reusing of the old, reflects sentiment as much as need. To discard something of value is waste, but also it is desecration.

It can be no accident that the Golden Age of the Yankee mechanics and full flowering of the storyteller's art were coeval in Maine. Each used bits and pieces of the old, embellishing to make the new; each was mindful of the past and sought to make it fit the present. Like hand skills, stories are hand-me-downs and have been passed along from generation to generation.

Folklore is a scholar's word. The great storytellers in the early decade of the present century were unaware that they were purveyors of oral history; the record of the Maine woods, or the days of sail, would be a thin broth indeed were it not for the tales told at lumber-camp Deacon Seats, in fo'c's'les of coasters and bankers, and related to rapt listeners gathered around the stoves of country stores.

Nor did the likes of O. A. Lombard, whose loghauler fathered the caterpillar tread, and Joe Peavey of Stillwater, whose name became the generic term for the cant dog that muckled untold millions of feet of timber, have any notion of their genius; they simply worked with bits and pieces and contrived something that would do the job at hand. Tinkers F. E. and F. O. Stanley of Kingfield concocted the Stanley Steamer from available odds and ends because the horse didn't go fast enough to suit them. For none of them was fortune the end dearly to be wished.

The woods of Maine were filled with unremembered haywire mechanics blessed with the knack of prolonging the usefulness of tools and machines. Time and patience and a respect for past endeavor were requisites for this art of making do. Planned obsolescence was a concept yet to be spawned by an age bent upon mass production and efficiency.

America has been moving in unseemly haste, wiping out its backtrail as it goes. A degree of affluence has been realized but at the cost of depersonalization and impoverishment of spirit. Like the mother with an alienated son, the nation is beginning to look backward to wonder where it went wrong. Perhaps only in northern New England does there remain living evidence of how it was. Maine is changing, but not yet has the past been plowed under and seeded over; here and there the old shows through the new like early coats of paint on a weathering barn.

The people of Maine are rememberers, and rememberers are storytellers. The lumber-camp Deacon Seat is gone and the country store is passing, yet the legends have not died. Maine remains a region of villages, and so long as there are villages there will be places to yarn and places to listen.

So long as rural life can withstand the blight of urbanization, there will be women who must improvise and men who must know a dozen skills to meet the challenges of each day; and there will be tinkerers, devisers, menders and reusers. And there will be attics, barns and sheds in which to gather the accumulations of the past; for like the storyteller's tales, this is the stuff of continuity, too good to be thrown away, too rich to be forgotten.

Maine Country Store

There was a time in living memory when the rural Maine village was a world unto itself. Huddled at the crossroads stood the school, the church, the Grange Hall and the store. Together, they served the simple needs of a simpler day.

The church and the Grange Hall remain perhaps, but the one-room school is gone; the store is no longer a general emporium, offering all worldly needs and serving also as the vital center of the social, political and economic life of the community.

With the coming of the Motor Age, distance ceases to be a limiting factor in the structure of society. As the village expands to become part of a larger sprawling world, its identity is weakened. What was once a lifetime place, self-contained, self-sufficient, wherein everyone knew everyone else, what they did, what they had and how they met good times and bad, is diminished as one by one the country stores close their doors, or are transformed into neighborhood markets.

Of man's five senses, smell is the most evocative. Childhood schooldays are recaptured in the scent of chalk dust, disinfectant and varnish; the smell of tarred rope can make a landlocked sailor weep. The smell of the country store defied analysis. It was a heady mixture of cheese, molasses, apples, tobacco, yard goods, leather, coffee, penny candy, enriched perhaps by effluvia of a wet dog or the customers around the potbellied stove.

These were honest odors, open and unapologetic. Little was sealed, wrapped or bottled. The wares were there in barrels, boxes or bins. You brought your own containers for vinegar, coal oil and molasses; and if you were lent a jug, you were expected to return it. And those six-for-a-penny candies—a heavenly choice of jaw-breakers, spruce gum, horehound drops and "lickerish" shoestrings—went from glass jars directly into small hands or were delivered in a twist of newspaper.

The store supplied other than worldly needs: it served as an escape from loneliness. ''When I was twelve I worked at my uncle's store,'' the Old Fellow recalls. ''Some of the men would walk in at night from the farms as much as four miles. They would sit around and talk and swap yarns; and then walk home again under the stars.

''They were like a part of my family, those old fellows. The women came to town maybe once a week. A man would come twice or three times a week in the winter, for then he had time on his hands. He'd buy a few things and maybe a newspaper, but what he really came for was company and men-talk. Don't know what those fellows would have done without the store.

''We sold mostly staples. Farmers raised their own pork and chicken. When the pork was gone by August and there wasn't enough chicken, save for Sundays, they went without meat. If a man could afford it, he might buy some steak cut thin to be served well-done with brown gravy. Of course there was always plenty of salt pork and potatoes. And there were kippers. They came in wooden boxes the size of an overnight suitcase. About half of what we traded went on the books. We didn't have many bad accounts. People paid when they could.''

In early Maine, settlement stores sprang up before schools and churches. These trading posts were the first expressions of community life. The first settlers weren't organized to grow all the produce they needed. At the store the farmer could trade what he had for what he required. The store served as a center for the exchange of goods and for the exchange of news, gossip and amenities as well.

These frontier stores were strictly family affairs and set up as a rule in the storekeeper's residence. The first crude homes were clustered, the men and boys going out each day from the settlements to outlying fields to tend their crops. During the Indian troubles which took up most of the first half of the eighteenth century, ''Indian Dogs,'' trained to sniff out any lurking redskin and give the alarm, accompanied the farmers.

The early storekeeper farmed on the side. Hay was often his staple crop, for hay could easily be bartered for eggs, chickens, beef and pork. Once the Indian wars were over, the farmers moved out onto their lands and the tight stockade aspects of community life gave way to a rural countryside, and the frontier interdependence gave way to some degree of individualism. Co-operation was still essential, for crops could not be harvested without some common effort, but the shape of an entrepreneurial society with its profit motive was discernible well before the American Revolution.

In many of the frontier settlements, the storekeeper served as the innkeeper. In some instances, the store was little more than an excuse for peddling ''West Indian Goods.'' One disapproving freeholder complained that the storekeeper ''kept a tippling place for a host of poor husbands like himself.''

Typically, though the early storekeeper was a man of substance and good repute. He was first of all a trader, and it behooved him to be a good one, for he dealt with a breed of good traders. The Yankee Levantine passion for the game has been explained as the Puritan substitute for gambling. There was a bit more to it than that. The scarcity of cash made trading a necessity. Some commodities had more or less fixed values: a sheep was worth a certain number of bushels of buckwheat, a certain count of split shingles bought a certain number of gallons of molasses. Other exchange values "floated" on the market, and trades depended upon scarcities and how badly a certain commodity was needed and what the traffic would bear.

The line between canniness and sharpness was obscure. If a fellow got a poor trade, the storekeeper was a rascal. When he made a good trade, his adversary was no more than canny. The storekeeper who made a good trade and sent the customer home thinking *he'd* got a good trade was a genius, and there were geniuses aplenty at the crossroads in nineteenth-century Maine.

The country storekeeper our fathers knew did more than run his establishment: he presided over it. He was called upon to adjudicate in matters of principle and referee when arguments became overheated. He usually found it expedient to keep his political affiliation a secret, particularly if he had Democratic leanings, although it was safe enough to be an avowed agnostic.

More often than not, the store housed the post office, the storekeeper acting as postmaster. No stickler for government regulations, he'd obligingly tuck messages in with the mail or pass them along verbally. The store served as an information and communications center, and every country store was plastered with notices and posters of upcoming events as well as lost-and-found bulletins. And in the early days of the telephone, the store frequently housed the one-and-only hand-cranked gadget in the region.

"I remember," the long-retired storekeeper said, "the first time Emmy Tilden called her daughter in Boston. She shouted into it so loud she could be heard in Appleton. Couldn't convince her she didn't need to shout to be heard all the way to Boston."

The country storekeeper was somewhat restricted in pricing staples, since the going price of such commodities as sugar, flour and dried beans was common knowledge. He had a little more to come and go on in general merchandise, and it was in this area that he exercised his Yankee talents. Most storekeepers had a secret code on the price tag which told the cost price of each item so they would know exactly just how much leeway there was for dickering.

"I was fair enough," the retired country storekeeper said. "If I thought I ought to get five dollars for a pair of boots, I'd price them at, say, five-fifty. If the customer looked interested and started feeling for his money but wasn't yet ready to let it go, I'd say, 'You been a good customer, John, let's make it an even five dollars.' We'd both feel good about that."

In many sections of rural Maine the farmer's wife had her small cache of "egg money" which she put aside for a new dress or something special. She would trade the eggs at the store to build up her equity on the books, or, commonly, the storekeeper would advance the dress so she could wear it while she was paying it off in eggs.

The St. John Valley was Maine's last frontier. Money was scarce to nonexistent well into the present century in that border country. The stores were trading posts and usually the sole centers of the social and economic life of the region. It was at the stores that the loggers and timber dealers gathered to trade, find or offer work, and exchange news and views.

Commonly, the storekeepers backed the stumpage contractors with grub and gear and took logs in payment in the spring. Many of the valley storekeepers made a pretty good thing of trading timber. Trespass cutting was a way of life along the Allagash and St. John rivers, and ''Moosetowners'' were a law unto themselves. More than a few storekeepers acted as middlemen for stolen timber. Since most of the timber cutters were on the storekeeper's books, accepting purloined timber was the simplest way to get the accounts cleaned up. It's estimated that a good half of the timber cut in that region between 1930 and 1950 was cut in the dead of night. In many cases, the big paper companies were buying their own timber from the storekeepers and they knew it; but they needed the logs and didn't dare be too fussy about the source of supply.

By all odds the most famous of Maine's general stores was D. T. Sanders & Son at Greenville. This woodsman's hallowed establishment at the foot of Moosehead Lake was founded in 1857, the year Henry David Thoreau took off from this spot on his final trip into the Maine woods. Greenville was the jumping-off place for woods-bound loggers, trappers and wilderness adventurers, and D.T. made the store renowned for stocking anything and everything a woods traveler could ask for.

There was little cash-and-carry for the simple reason there was little cash. Just about everything went down on ledgers. The store would carry trappers and loggers over the winter, and they would pay off their accounts when they got paid in the spring. During the money panic in the 1880s, D.T. did better than that. The Sanders store issued scrip that circulated freely in the town so that life and business could ride out the emergency.

On the occasion of the store's centennial in 1957, Harry Sanders, grandson of the founder, reminisced about the early days. ''Sanders' store was the information center for the whole area. There had to be someplace where a fellow could go to find out when the next stage left or when some logger or trapper was expected out of the woods. Both my father and grandfather made it a business to be obliging. They were both careful with their pennies, though. You know, for years they took one paper between them, the old Bangor *Commercial*, a weekly then. They would take turns, one reading it first one week, the other getting first whack at it the next.''

A good many country stores found themselves in the banking business in nineteenth-century Maine. It was a long way between banks, and the ones available were suspect by rural people. Loans backed by good security and carrying whatever interest the traffic would bear offered a nice little sideline for the storekeeper with capital. And sometimes a storekeeper without capital found a shrewd way to keep his head above water.

One canny old-timer explained his method of marginal banking. ''Say a fellow had a contract to cut five thousand cord of pulpwood over the winter. I'd carry him on the books for what he needed, and in the spring he'd present the check he got for the wood. I'd subtract what he owed me and give him the balance in small checks of not more than twenty dollars. He'd cash those checks one at a time as he needed money and over a period of as much as a year. In the meantime, I'd have interest-free use of that money and get thanked for my service in the bargain.''

The Madison Avenue adman could have learned a thing or two about human psychology from the old-time Maine storekeeper. In *Yankee Storekeeper*, Ralph Gould tells of a lesson he learned as a boy from his first boss. ''He took me aside the first day I went to work for him. 'Boy,' he said, 'when you weigh out a bag of sugar, always have less than the full amount in the bag when you put it on the scales. Then put in a bit more to make the weight right. That pleases the customer. If he sees you take a little bit out to make it right, that makes him mad.' ''

Maine was a prohibition state a half century before the Volstead Act. Maine people accommodated themselves to the drought in a characteristic manner: they did with what they had. Some storekeepers managed to feign amazement at the amount of vanilla extract that was sold across their counters, despite the common knowledge that the stuff was 90 per cent alcohol. And there were those who salved their consciences by maintaining two prices: one price for cooking purposes, and a higher price for drinking. It was fairly obvious that a fellow who asked for a dozen bottles wasn't buying it for his wife's kitchen.

The storekeeper over Anson way was a stickler for legality. He made a point of asking the customer how the vanilla was to be used before he passed it over. In line with his practice, he asked the French Canadian who wanted two-dozen bottles of vanilla what he wanted it for.

''My wife she's wan to make one hell of a big Nova Scotia cake,'' the Frenchman said blandly.

The storekeeper was every bit as bland. ''Be a shame, Émile, to hold up a big cake like that,'' he said. ''Same time, it'd be more of a shame to have your wife go to all that trouble and then find you too almighty drunk to enjoy it.''

Maine Town Meeting

According to the annals, the first town meeting in Camden, Maine, convened in the spring of 1791. Duly warned, thirty-two freeholders gathered at Peter Ott's Tavern. Affable William Gregory was named Moderator. John Harkness, a bookish fellow and a veteran of the recent War of Independence, was elected Town Clerk and First Selectman. From all accounts, the meeting was brief, informal and without rancor.

The main business of the day was to assume self-government. Since there were more offices than citizens to fill them, the more knowledgeable settlers were forced to double in brass. In addition to three Selectmen, the slate called for a Constable, Tax Collector, Treasurer, a panel of Surveyors of Highways, a number of Fence

Viewers, Surveyors of Lumber and Cullers of Staves, Tythingmen, Sealers of Leather, a Sealer of Weights and Measures, and a Pound Keeper.

Aside from the problem of highways, or rather the lack of them, the most pressing issue was vagrant livestock. As New England poet Robert Frost noted much later, "good fences make good neighbors." It was voted to pay Robert Thorndike three pounds "to build a pound on Peter Ott's land and Peter Ott to be Pound Keeper." The said pound was to be "seven feet high and tight enough to stop pigs a month old."

The Maine town meeting hasn't changed appreciably in form and purpose over the centuries. In those early years, the privilege of voting was limited to those male citizens "being twenty-one years of age, a resident of said town for a space of a year and having freehold estate within said town of the annual income of three pounds or any estate to the value of sixty pounds," but such qualifying limitations weren't all that restrictive or discriminatory. Our distaff ancestors had no wish to be party to the coarse rough-and-tumble those early meetings often provided. And the property requirement excluded no more than a handful of shiftless indigents.

Then, as today, the posted warrant "warned" the citizens to meet at a designated time and place and to act upon a list of articles. The usage is apt. The voters are given fair warning to turn out and participate in local government or hold their peace until another spring rolls around.

And turn out they do, rain or shine, in sickness or in health. A dull state or federal election may bring out only the party faithful. Everybody turns out for a Maine town meeting. Nothing that goes on in Washington can divert interest from such contentious local issues as, say, the question of whether the decrepit old Town Hall should be torn down or restored, or a new piece of fire-fighting equipment purchased.

The town meeting is peculiar to New England. And downright peculiar it must seem to the uninitiated stranger if he fails to grasp that this annual spring event is much more than a political function; that it has strong social and tribal overtones which carry it well into the realm of a folkway.

A lot of nonsense has been written about the Maine town meeting. It has been called "democracy's last stronghold" and "the ultimate expression of self-government." *Life* magazine, a while back, termed it "the quintessence of Democracy." Meeting Day does indeed afford the citizens of Maine towns the opportunity to speak their minds and to vote directly on matters that affect their lives, but that's only a part of the reason they turn out joyfully and en masse. Maine people turn out to town meetings because everybody turns out to town meetings and no one wants to miss anything. And this has been going on a long time.

There is nothing solemn about a Maine town meeting. A typical gathering combines the best features of Old Home Week, an Odd Fellows' Barbecue and an encounter between a Hatfield and a McCoy. It's a time to renew acquaintances after a long, hard winter. The men swap yarns, the ladies exchange recipes and symptoms, and one and all get caught up on the gossip. A good fight on the floor isn't necessary for full enjoyment, but it helps. March is the beginning of mud season in Maine, and any diversion on the long downhill slide to a laggard spring is gratefully received.

For all its country-fair atmosphere, the Maine town meeting is not a frivolous affair. Maine people have a passion for local autonomy and are jealous of the right to govern themselves as they see fit. When a state of emergency arose in the early days, it was the towns themselves that decided how many fighting men would be mustered and how much would be raised for ball and powder. And often it was decided locally which provincial laws should be obeyed and which ones ignored.

This self-reliance was bred of necessity. Settlements were far apart and communication between them tenuous. The tagline of that old Maine yarn "you can't get there from here" wasn't necessarily a joke. Roads have improved since then, but attitudes concerning a town's integrity have been altered only slightly by time. The presence of a citizen of a neighboring village is suffered, but if he wants to speak from the floor, he must first have the assent of the entire assemblage.

Traditionally, Maine town meetings are held in March. Putting the date off until April would be safer weatherwise, certainly, but the delay might well exacerbate the late-winter malaise. Maine people, disposed as they are to be neighborly, can get a bit owly after the long winter. March is none too soon to get out, rub elbows and let off a little steam.

Until recent years a Maine town meeting was called to order at nine or ten in the morning and continued all day, with a break for lunch put on by the church or Grange ladies. The Moderator would wind up the morning proceedings adroitly when word got to him that the beans were ready. Latterly, many Maine towns have opted for night meetings, a trend which inevitably will diminish the holiday air of these occasions.

As one old-timer put it, "Could be night meetings bring out a few more people and a few less town dogs. And Bill Gregory, who usually takes the floor to talk about the Old Days till the cows come home, is getting a mite too old to come out nights, and that sure is a blessing."

Whether convened by night or by day, these hallowed rites of spring call the Maine citizenry to bare, wind-beleaguered halls as bees to the hive. Inevitably, the hall is either too hot or too cold, depending on the vagaries of the ancient furnace or the disposition of the janitor. The ladies come in their Sunday best; the men, less inclined to sartorial display, come as they are for the most part and in the clothes of their trades: wool shirts, garage jumpers, work pants and gunning caps. You see a dappling of white shirts and ties, but hardly enough to lend a truly churchly atmosphere to the gathering.

The Moderator is wearing a tie, of course. He won't officially be named until the gavel brings the meeting to order, but his election is preordained. The qualifications for this post are rather special: a good Moderator should know everybody in town, be respected, fair yet firm, and possess at least an operational knowledge of parliamentary law. Once a citizen both capable and willing is found, he can count on the job until health or infirmity intervenes.

Once the Moderator has assumed the podium, the next piece of business before the meeting is the election of town officers. Since the Selectmen's terms are staggered, it's usually a matter of filling one or perhaps two vacancies on the board. More often than not, this comes down to the re-election of incumbents. A big problem in Maine towns is to get a qualified citizen to take the job. Now and again, the situation arises where a fellow who had the job doesn't want any more of it. The money is minimal, and the dubious honor doesn't balance off the headaches the Selectman's post entails.

Curiously, the fellow who really wants the job and goes after it with high-pressure electioneering methods is least likely to succeed. His zeal is suspect, particularly if he's new in town. Typically, a candidate makes himself available only after being prevailed upon by friends who are concerned that some willing newcomer might get elected if some qualified citizen—that is to say, someone who doesn't really want the job—fails to step forward.

Campaigning for any local post is strictly low pressure. Maine people take their own sweet time to make up their minds, but once their minds are made up, no amount of golden oratory is going to change them. In a small Maine town where everyone knows everyone, it's common knowledge where certain clans and individuals stand on a given issue. There are those who vote consistently against anything that entails spending money, and there are those who can be counted on to vote against anything proposed by "those new people." And there is always that stubborn coterie which doesn't wish to be beholden to anyone and votes solidly and perpetually against accepting state and federal funds for any purpose.

Actually, appropriations of big money for such things as roads and schools are usually passed without any great fuss. It is those questions that bear directly upon individual rights such as zoning which create the commotion. And recently, proposed dog-leash ordinances have been responsible for some lively free-for-alls.

Maine towns have practiced self-government for a couple of centuries. They have learned to respect the rules of the game. When things get a bit out of hand, a mild rebuke from the Moderator—"Billy, you're way out of order, so why don't you just sit down and keep quiet"—is usually sufficient to get the meeting back on the track.

The outlander's common view of the Maine town meeting as a "forum for public debate" is also a possible exaggeration. Generally, there is little need for extended debate on the floor of the meeting, since most questions are thrashed out on street corners and in front of the post office well in advance.

The emotional issues are seldom resolved on the streets, however. It may be pegged as a truism that Maine voters are more apt to turn out and vote *against* something than *for* something. Those who hope to put something across are aware of this contrary strain; they keep their voices low so as not to arouse the opposition.

There may be a bit of probing and airing of a polarizing issue in the weeks preceding the town meeting, but the exploration is handled gingerly. Much better to lie low and plan a little quiet strategy. A favorite ploy exercised by the opposition is to designate someone to get the floor the moment the article is read to move that the article be passed over. This sometimes takes the proponents by surprise, and the motion to kill the article is carried before they can get an oar in.

Commonly, both sides dragoon respected citizens into rising and stating their positions. The shrewd advocate is careful not to go beyond the simple statement of his personal views. Any attempt to instruct voters on how they should vote is counterproductive.

Finding good advocates who will take the floor and state their views is no great problem; the really sticky proposition is to keep the wrong ones in their seats. Every Maine town is burdened with a few abrasive characters who insist upon being heard and whose support can amount to a kiss of death.

A seasoned town-meeting-goer can spot the fireworks in any town warrant at a glance. Most articles carry a ''yes'' or ''no'' recommendation by the Board of Selectmen or the Budget Committee. Invariably, the controversial articles are appended with a ''no recommendation.'' Maine town officers are not crazy. They choose the better part of valor and, as the warrant phrasing goes, ''see what the town will do about it.''

The term ''town fathers'' suggests the ingredient of paternalism in the structure of Maine town government. If the term ''paternal and benevolent oligarchy'' may be used loosely, that about sums up the political nature of a Maine town. The typical small Maine town is run by a handful of citizens most of whom consider the interests of the town above their own. Members of this cadre may never run for office, but they do have a great deal to say about who gets elected.

This by no means suggests that those who do make it become creatures of the leadership group. The system which operates to thwart such subversion of the democratic process has never been enunciated and is possibly only dimly perceived. Most small Maine towns have no more than a score or so who qualify as acceptable candidates for the Board of Selectmen. This constitutes what might be termed the Selectman Pool. Each year, there is at least one incumbent on the board whose sins of omission or commission have alienated enough of the electorate to get himself in the doghouse. He either steps down or is voted out and his place taken by another from the Pool.

By the time the next spring has rolled around, these real or imagined sins are likely forgotten. Maine people are reasonably tolerant of human erring. Except in the area of frugality and the work ethic, they are not laden with too many Puritan hangups. Sin is a human condition. Deplorable it may be, but Maine people have an intuitive knowledge that sin will always be with us and we might as well learn to live with it. They also realize that if a little sinning disqualified a fellow from serving the town, they'd have the devil's own time finding anyone to serve.

Thus, the once rejected town father usually will be voted back on the board, if he so wishes. There's a place for him, of course. By that time there is bound to be another incumbent who has offended. This fellow simply steps down and takes last year's sinner's place in the doghouse, there to bide his time.

Since no two Maine towns are alike, there are any number of variations of this political *modus operandi,* but basically the process is the same. This may not be "pure democracy," but it works very well.

Back a few decades before many Maine towns opted for the hiring of town managers, the First Selectman was truly the town father, and in some cases an old-fashioned paterfamilias at that. Arthur Walker, until his death at the age of eighty-plus, served as Rockport's First Selectman for twenty-five years. Arthur ran things his own way and pretty much single-handed. For a quarter of a century he was as much a fixture at town meetings as the American flag on the bare stage. He possessed only a part of one arm. Invariably, he sat in the third row of the Town Hall, and what town business he didn't carry in his head he held tucked under the stub of his truncated member.

Arthur was inclined to be a bit arbitrary, but he was unfailingly responsive to the problems of his flock. When a backcountry farmer wanted to know why the snowplow didn't get through to him, he would call Arthur and that plow would get through somehow. Or if some citizen had a dog in his sheep pasture, Arthur would see to it that something was done about it personally and promptly.

Arthur possessed most of the virtues and some of the weaknesses that make up an ideal town father. He was canny, thrifty and practical. He had a Yankee abhorrence of sloth, but if a town charge was snowed in without food, he'd break trail to his house with the needed provisions. The year he couldn't hire anyone to "honey dip" the poor-farm septic tank, he went out and did it himself. A carpenter by trade, he saw no reason why the town should pay good money to hire a carpenter to repair and rehang the town sign the day it blew down. He got out his ladder and did the job personally.

Though a strong and faithful Baptist by persuasion, Arthur had the good sense to accommodate himself to a little sin and corruption rather than upset deep-grooved customs. He knew perfectly well why Henry, who drove the town snowplow, saw to it that Sam Miller got his road plowed promptly. It was because Sam saw to it that the bung was off his hard-cider barrel. And Henry was obliging when a friend suggested that he might as well patch up his private drive so long as he was on the street with the tar truck. Not only did Henry like to help out a friend; he also liked the bottle of hard stuff he could expect at Christmas.

Arthur was forever threatening to retire, but he never did get around to it. Naturally there was some muttering as this one-man rule extended over several decades. Some said he was a bit too cozy with the summer people and worked in their behalf. On the other hand, either by his charm or perhaps because his position as Tax Assessor gave him some leverage, he managed to wheedle more gifts for the town from the summer folk than anyone thought possible.

This ancient town-meeting form of government has its weaknesses. It must seem a bit bizarre to city people who leave it to surrogate councilmen to handle the details of civic management, that a whole hall full of voters should be permitted to haggle for hours over a question of spraying or not spraying trees or whether or not a new streetlight should be installed on Mrs. Grundy's corner.

Admittedly, such a process is cumbersome, inefficient and at times a bit enervating. On the other hand, citizens who can speak out even in a losing cause seldom experience the frustrations which afflict the majority of Americans, who never have direct confrontations with those they elect to serve them. Some Maine towns are run better than others, but it is fair to say that only under the town-meeting form of government do the people truly get the government they deserve.

Yet for all such lofty imputations, the Maine town meeting might have withered away long since were it not for the human, down-to-earth pleasure it brings to those who participate. Maine people turn out for town meetings because they enjoy them.

The unexpected may happen at a town meeting, but it is the pleasure of fulfilled expectations that sustains and perpetuates this sociopolitical folkway. Like the Passion Play or the classic Western, the Maine town meeting is essentially a reenactment. The actors may change with the passing years, but the roles are timeless. Civic conscience is always there in some local personification, as is the devil's advocate. The latter appears in various guises, most commonly in the person of a smooth-talking newcomer plumping for deficit spending or the acceptance of federal funding for some unneeded furbelow.

And inevitably, there is on the scene the town wit for comic relief and the windy oldster who dwells endlessly upon the glories of the Good Old Days. Most towns have a Crazy Mary and a Simple Simon and they, too, are accepted as supernumeraries in a familiar drama.

Whatever a town meeting is, no one could call it an outworn or perfunctory exercise. It may well be "democracy's last stronghold," but no sensible State-of-Mainer would encourage that pompous notion for fear he'd be obliged to wear a necktie. At its best, the town meeting demonstrates eternal political vigilance and a healthy insistence upon accountability. At the least, as Charlie Poore put it one recent spring, "It's one hell of a lot more fun than staying home and looking at television."

The Maine Language and the One-Room School

E. B. White commented perceptively on Maine folkways when he first settled here in the late thirties. The Maine way of life suited him fine, but he had difficulty with the language. His boy had trouble, too. White wrote: "Our boy came home from school the first day and said the school was peachy, but he couldn't understand what anybody was saying."

The boy got the hang of it soon enough. One was forced to sink or swim with eight grades in a one-room school, and a one-room school was about all rural Maine had to offer a few decades back.

A sizable segment of the state population now in its middle years had its introduction to learning in these country institutions. And in the back eddies of Maine and on some off-shore islands the one-room school still carries on, complete with potbellied stove and an all-purpose, no-nonsense schoolmarm.

The one-room-school marm of the recent past was all Maine and a yard wide. Maine had no need to import teachers; the state had a surplus of native pedagogues. In fact, there was a time when teachers were one of the state's most valuable exports. The one-room-school marm was usually a neighbor. The youngsters were taught to read and write standard English, but what they spoke was the vulgate of their particular bailiwick. Like a jaybird, a Maine native is easily identified when he opens his mouth, yet by no means is speech standard along the coast. Until the bridge connected Deer Isle with the mainland a few decades back, the islanders spoke a language that sounded exotic even to Maine off-islanders. Some scholars suggest that the phrasing and syntactical habits of isolated coastal populations may offer clues to the origins of the English language in America. It might well be that the speech patterns heard in the one-room-school yards in isolated Maine backwaters were little-corrupted seventeenth-century West Country English.

The children of Finnish immigrants and other ethnic groups that moved into Maine in the early decade of this century had a difficult time with the strange language. And even those with English-speaking backgrounds had problems of communication. Pity the poor youngster when he first came up against a *laud of dressin'*. He might have grasped that a *laud* is a load; but how was he expected to know that there was no such thing as manure in Maine. Nor is there today such a thing as loam. If you are making a new lawn, what you order is a *laud of loom*. And a fish trap is not a weir, but a *ware*.

The Maine speech has remained relatively uncluttered with the neologisms which are corrupting the standard American language. Honed by time and use, it is as clean and spare as the lines of a bank dory. *Bigness* is a fine Maine word. When a Maine farmer says his house is about the bigness of a neighbor's barn, the analogy has a fine resonance.

And take the word *heft*. You heft something to test its weight. First, of course, you take *aholt* of it. Then, there's the word *tunk*. To tunk something you give it a light tap, say, with a hammer. A carpenter might say to his partner who is fitting a window, "Tunk it a mite, she needs to go just a whisker." Not a little, not a fraction—a *whisker*.

When a Maine trout fisherman sets out, he takes his tackle box, sure enough; but when he's using a block and fall, what he's using is a *taykle*. And he never hoists anything; he *hists* it. A common syntactical Maine-ism favored by schoolchildren and which went uncorrected by one-room-school marms was *so didn't I* for "I didn't either.'' One can only suppose that that was the way this agreement was uttered in another century. This may also be said of the Maine school youngster's *dasn't*.

Take the use in Maine of a simple adjective as an adverb. A sinner is seldom characterized as wicked. The weather, though, may be *wicked* hot or *wicked* cold. And a man may be *wicked* poor. Both Chaucer and Shakespeare slipped into such usage without apology.

Such regional usage is both expressive and clear and should pose no great communication problem. The Maine broad *a* and the elision of the *r* can be a bit troublesome to the stranger, however. *Famine* isn't necessarily one of the Four Horsemen: in Maine, it can be something a farmer does when he works his piece. And there are words so special to Maine that they require translation. Take the word *dozy*. A junk of wood that's rotten and not fit to burn is dozy. *Junk* of wood? It's always a *junk* of wood or a *junk* of meat in Maine. Not piece. Not hunk. *Junk*.

And then there's the Maine word *gaumy*. The fellow moving a piano might find it gaumy, or awkward to handle. And a growing boy, all feet and arms, is also gaumy. And the fellow moving that piano will not tilt it to get it through the doorway, he'll *cant* it.

Summer people and the new homesteaders are prone to err in their attempts to pick up the Maine lingo. Natives do not say ''State o' Maine.'' *State-a-Maine* does the trick. And a storm from a north quarter is not a nor'easter; it's a *no'theaster*. A good stiff breeze is simply a *blow* or a *gale of wind*.

A host of other salty archaisms persist along the coast. A *mug-up* is a coffee break. Fishermen who meet up offshore and stop to visit are *gamming*, a usage inherited from the Yankee whaling days. On a trawlerman's good days everything is the *finest kind*. Then, there are days when trawls get fouled up on the bottom and nets are *rimwracked*. Anything damaged, fouled up or on its last legs is said to be rimwracked in Maine parlance. A *gunkhole* is a quiet cove or anchorage and the word is sometimes used as a verb: to go *gunkholing* is to cruise casually with no definite objective.

Few outside of Maine have ever heard of *puckerbrush*. This is the hunter-woodsman term for thick stands of birch or poplar, or any thicket that resists passage. And poplar is usually *popple*, and there is no such thing as a larch—it's *hackmatack*. To compound the confusion, coastal boatbuilders who use this wood for ships' *knees* call it *juniper*.

Since Maine is a wildlife state, inevitably outdoorsmen have contributed their share to the enrichment of the Maine language. Before the century's turn, the out-of-state hunter and fisherman was a *sporter*. Today this has been simplified to *sport*. A Maine man goes *gunnin'* unless it's deer he's after, in which case he goes *deer huntin'*. And it may come as a surprise to the uninitiated that Maine people seldom, if ever, eat venison: they consume *deer meat* aplenty, however.

Among the old usages persisting in the Maine outdoorsman's lexicon is the word *biddable.* A working dog that is obedient is biddable. Decoys are always *tollers*. And when a fisherman tosses bait upon the water to attract fish around his boat, he's not chumming, but *using toll bait*. And there is another special use for the word *bait* in Maine. That junk of wood or rock the fellow shoves near the end of his fulcrum when he's prizing with a crowbar is referred to as *bait*.

There are words and phrases frequently employed for flavor by those *from away* who like to think they've got the feel of the Maine lingo. Ever since the conversational affirmation *ayeh* has become the outlander's code for Maine talk, natives have tended to shy away from it. It is certainly true, though, that Mainers are *mod'rate* in the use of their lips. One explanation for this laziness, for what it's worth, is that Maine winters being what they are, lips tend to get *froze up*.

It's pretty much a thing of the past for State-of-Mainers to go *up to Boston*. In the old sailing days, Down East skippers did indeed sail *up to Boston* against the prevailing westerlies and downwind or down east on the voyage home to Maine. Today, Maine Yankees sensibly go *down to Boston*, is only to avoid being thought of as quaint. Most emphatically, Maine people are not fussy about being thought of as quaint. It should be explained that when a Mainer says he is not fussy about something, this means that he is.

Logging in its Golden Age contributed some fine words and imagery to the Maine tongue. When rocks are bared by low water, the river is said to be *bony*. The fellow not overambitious is called a *bank beaver*, deriving from the beaver that settles for a hole in the bank rather than contribute to the building of a lodge. The old logging-camp words *haywire* and *fink* are today standard Americanisms. Their Maine attribution may be arguable, but certainly *haywire* meaning busted, crazy or flimsy, and *fink* meaning stoolie or company man, were in Maine woods use a good half century before they were in national currency.

An early writer on the American language noted that there was a greater difference in dialect between one county and another in Britain than there was between one state and another in America. He assigned as a reason the fact that Americans move frequently from place to place "and are not liable to local peculiarities in accents or phraseology."

Maine people, particularly rural people, are not addicted to this characteristic American roaming habit, which could account for Maine's speech individuality. Most State-of-Mainers would not accept that they speak a dialect, while they freely, even firmly, would agree that there is a Maine way of talking. Moreover, they would be inclined to consider the difference a distinction rather than an anomaly.

Lowell, in his *Bigelow Papers*, acknowledged the existence of the Yankee vulgate and genially offered a few pointers for the uninitiated. Among the "General Rules" he mentioned that "the genuine Yankee never gives the rough sound to the *r* when he can help it, and in fact displays considerable ingenuity in avoiding it even before a vowel. . . . He seldom sounds the final *g*, a piece of self-denial, if we consider his partiality for nasals."

Although Lowell's observations have a peripheral application to Maine, Maine people—if one may except a small coterie of landed "old-money gentry" who identify more with Boston and Harvard than with Maine—do not speak the standard New England dialect. Maine early was isolated from the Commonwealth and antipathetic to its culture. While Maine did draw some settlers from Massachusetts, primarily of west and south English blood, a sizable portion of the early Maine pioneers were Scotch-Irish who came from North England and brought with them the speech rhythms and syntactical habits that persist in Maine to this day.

The one-room school, where oral Maine language was acquired, was modern in many of its aspects. The students learned pretty much at their own speed and advanced according to their individual aptitudes. The eight grades were usually arranged in three groups—young, intermediate and older students. The children shifted from group to group, taking arithmetic with one, reading and spelling with another, and geography with the third, according to the individual's development. There were few tests or examinations and little homework. The schoolday went from nine in the morning until four in the afternoon, and with the burden of home chores there was little time left for extracurricular assignments.

Wrote Lura Beam about the one-room school she knew as a child, "The pupil paid no attention to the class below his own level, just as the accustomed ear does not hear the commercials, but he followed everything above his level thirstily, as if it were a much more valuable message than his own work. Knowledge was made to seem a lofty reality, vastly remote, yet priceless. The one-room school conveyed a feeling that learning was better than other things."

Inevitably, Maine is feeling the effect of the leveling forces at work in America today. The steady impact of movies, television and those other manifestations of mass communication is grinding away at the stubborn hillocks of nonconformity. The old one-room school has given way to the consolidated school, manned more and more frequently by out-of-state teachers with their predilection for standard American speech. Maine colleges are becoming more and more cosmopolitan, and the youth of Maine are increasingly seeking a taste of the world beyond Maine's borders. For better or worse, the one-room school is vanishing, and the country lad's dawdling walk home through woods and across fields is being pre-empted by the yellow bus. The day may come when strangers from away will understand the Maine schoolboy's lingo, and the sound of the Yankee *a* will no longer be heard in the land.

That day will not come soon. Maine speech is deeply rooted and as resistant to erosion as the country rock of its coast. It will be yet a while before a Maine schoolboy will stoop to spread manure upon his father's acres. Maine winters will continue to be wicked cold and summers wicked hot for a long and grateful time to come.

The Maine Finn

The language and the culture of the English-shaped Maine society in its beginnings and the Anglo-Saxon stamp remain upon this northern land. Yet Maine, like the nation, is a distillate of disparate breeds and bloods. The common notion of Maine's relative ethnic purity is a myth.

To the bloodlines of the first settlers, add those of the Indian, French, Irish, Greek, Italian, Norwegian, Swede, Pole, Russian and Finn. All are here today, and with the possible exception of the French, indistinguishable in their attitudes and values from the native stock.

Certainly Maine was not a "melting pot" in the sense that these ethnic ingredients were stirred together to produce an American archetype. What has emerged from the process of acculturization are products as various as their racial strains, yet somehow revealing in common those traits traditionally associated with the Maine character. Americans they may be; but first of all they are State-of-Mainers. These immigrant villages have not so much altered the special qualities of the state as they have confirmed and strengthened them.

Consider the Maine Finns. The broad face, square jaw, the slightly Eurasian cast of the eyes, may betray their origin as do the names—Ruohomaa, Piirtinen, Ilvonen, Harjula; but today these second- and third-generation State-of-Mainers appear as Yankee as fish chowder. They adapted quickly because from the beginning they belonged to Maine.

These North European people were a part of the great tide of immigration which reached American shores in the decades between the Civil War and the First World War. In the course of this migration, some four hundred thousand Finns discovered the New World.

The ports of Boston and New York received the bulk of the Finnish immigrants. They funneled out of these cities to the mining and timbering regions of North Central United States, upper New York State, the mill and quarry towns of Massachusetts. They came with little more than hope and the clothes on their backs.

They were a tough, proud and self-reliant breed. A constitutional heritage and the conditioning of a cold, austere land had made them so. The Finns have a word for it: *sisu*. Loosely translated, it comes out perseverance, courage and stamina; or perhaps more earthily, guts with a touch of stubbornness.

And they needed all of this, for as the Finnish anti-emigration literature of the times warned, "Even in America one cannot whittle gold with a wooden knife. With your sweated brow you must eat your bread."

Through the centuries of precarious history, the Finns have been invaded, threatened and partitioned by powerful neighbors. With Russia alone, Finland has fought a dozen wars—and lost all of them. Prior to her domination by Russia, Finland had been ruled by Sweden for six hundred and fifty years. The independence she gained in 1917 was final fulfilment for a freedom-loving people.

The major force compelling emigration was the desperate condition of the Finnish economy, which exerted an oppressive hardship upon the large and landless agricultural working class. A contributing factor was a deep aversion to conscription of Finns by the Russian Army. Then, of course, there were the restless ones, offspring of the more privileged landed class, who left to seek adventure. And there were many who fretted under the stricture of the stern National Lutheran Church.

The Finns call their fatherland *Suomi*, a word not even a Finn can explain. The Finnish people possess a strong feeling of national identity born of centuries of adversity. When the Russian hordes invaded Finland in 1939, the Finns exclaimed in mock dismay, "Where will we bury them all?" This dark inward-turned laughter has been the rod and the staff of Finnish survival.

Few in the initial wave of Finnish immigrants came directly to Maine. There was a ready market for raw labor in the Massachusetts quarry and mill towns. Maine was to get her small share of Finns as the new century opened. In June of 1938, when the Finns of Maine took part in the national Finnish celebration to commemorate the tercentenary of the landing in Delaware of the first Finn pioneers, it was estimated that five thousand Finns lived within Maine boundaries, a thousand in villages of the Rockland region alone.

The first Finnish settlement in Maine of any consequence was at Long Cove on the so-called "Georges River Road," which runs seaward from Thomaston to Port Clyde. The first Finns trickled into this region shortly after the Civil War. By 1887 there were perhaps a dozen Finnish families at Long Cove and along the River Road, among them the Hahls, Harjulas, the Honnkonens. The great influx began around 1895 and continued until after the Depression years when improving economic conditions in Finland, the lessening of opportunities for raw labor here, and the tightening of U.S. immigration restrictions staunched the flow.

It was the granite that brought them here. The quarries at Long Cove and on the Penobscot Bay islands of Vinalhaven and Hurricane were booming. The cities were crying for paving blocks. The Maine quarry owners were knee-deep in back orders. Many other ethnic groups were involved: Swedes, Scots, Irish, Italians, Welsh; but it was the Finns who bore the main burden of cutting granite from the earth. It was estimated that 40 per cent of the quarry work force were newly settled Finns.

By 1910, the Finns of the River Road were pulling themselves out of the mire of economic peonage. They were taking the first steps from nothing to something. The Finns who came to Maine had a deep and abiding love of the land and the independence ownership of land offered. They were buying up the old farms abandoned as submarginal by the early stock. They were restoring the farmhouses, and with bone labor they were bringing the land back to productivity. By 1920, virtually every mailbox along the River Road had a Finnish name scrawled upon it.

The story of the Finns on the Penobscot islands of Vinalhaven and Hurricane followed much the same pattern. The young Finns, escaping the dire economic conditions and the growing fear of Russification, sought work in the New World. The guidebooks and the bulletins told them where work could be found. Many worked first in the quarry towns of Massachusetts. Lockouts and layoffs in the Massachusetts quarries sent them to Maine.

The inducements offered were often hyperbolic and hand-tailored to appeal to the Finnish national. What Finn could resist ''a veritable Eden,'' a region ''blessed with beautiful nature, healthful atmosphere . . . a land safe from cyclones, snowslides, hailstorms and poisonous snakes''?

The granite boom began on Hurricane Island in 1870 when Civil War General Davis Tillson started operations. The granite was prime and the demand so great that almost overnight a town sprang up. In flocked the Finns, the Swedes, Scots, Italians and Irish, a landless, migrant army of new Americans seeking no more than a survival wage. The Scots and the Swedes frequently came with skills learned abroad. The Finns, for the most part, were forced to start at the bottom and learn the trade.

A woman recalling her childhood on the island at the turn of the century wrote, ''I've heard tell there used to be a lot of prejudice against foreigners in Maine towns. There wasn't any on Hurricane. Maybe it was because we were stuck off at sea all working granite and sharing hard times. There was a building called Anarchist Hall where the workers met and played cards and drank wine and listened to the Finns talk about unions and co-operatives. The Finns were great people for whistling up a quarryman's courage with brave talk of good times ahead.''

The men who worked the granite needed brave talk. When the Finns who had come alone called for their families, there soon were many mouths to feed and not enough in the pay envelope to cover anything beyond subsistence. The writer recalls, ''All of us of different tongues went to the same school to learn English and to read and write, the older ones helping the younger ones. But we got by somehow, although the best even a stonecutter could make was one-dollar-fifty a day. It was a hard life doubtless, but it made men strong, tougher than horses some of them were.''

The Finns who settled backcountry in the region of Rockland arrived in Maine somewhat later than the raw, unskilled quarry workers of Long Cove and the islands. They had left Finland for the same reasons. What made them different was the advanced state of their acculturization. Most of the Finns who settled in the hills of Knox and Lincoln counties in the first decades of the twentieth century had, by the time they reached Maine, acquired a little English, and some had even put by a little money. A very little is all they had of either, but it was enough to set them apart from the quarry workers.

The Finns in the back hills of Knox County tended to be freethinkers. Or perhaps they expressed a certain native pragmatism. They felt no need ''to go to church, pay a preacher's salary or sweat in the company of a catechism at a reading examination in Free America.''

Earl Tolman, whose family was settled in the region of West Rockport before the Revolution, confirms this anticlericalism. ''The Finns that settled here in Rockport never went to church, to my knowledge. But they were good people. Fine people. They were hard-working, honest. A Finn would come to my father,'' Earl Tolman recalls, '' 'need a cow,' he would say, 'got no money.' Finns were never turned down. They would pay off what they owed by working for my father or pay him off a little at a time. The local farmers might have been suspicious at first, but they soon learned that the Finn's word was his bond."

The thing that struck the Yankee farmers most forcibly was the work load assumed by the women in a Finnish family. "The Finn women cooked, sewed and worked in the fields with their men," Earl Tolman remembers, "and some were in the field a few hours before their babies were born. The men were the bosses in the Finnish family, but it was the women that held the families together. If it hadn't been for their women, I don't think the Finns would have made it here."

Those backcountry Finns required something more than a passion for hard work; they needed a little luck to make it. And a little luck fell their way. The Finns are a race of woodcutters. They went at clearing the overgrown farms with ax and saw. The lime kilns in Rockport village were in desperate need of wood to fire the kilns. This was the cash crop that saved the Rockport Finns in those early years of their settlement.

And when the land was cleared, sunlight released the blueberries. It was like an answer to a prayer. The Finns quickly learned the little there was to know about blueberry husbandry. In all that region of West Rockport and Warren, blueberries became the cash crop. This was a crop that required whole families in dawn-to-dusk labor. Two generations of Finns prospered.

The Finn blueberry growers were small operators, for the most part. But there were a few blueberry kings—notably Mikko Lofman and Selim Ruohomaa, whose only child, Kosti, was to become a world-famous photographer and whose love of the land was reflected in his telling work. And with the coming of blueberries, co-operatives came to Maine.

The co-operative was one of the most significant characteristics of the Finnish enclaves in Maine. Many factors were responsible for the remarkable growth of Finnish immigrant co-operative enterprise. To begin with, there was a strong, deep-rooted ideological basis for the Finnish attraction to this movement. Most of the co-ops were born and nurtured in militant socialism and the early union movement. The granite workers talked over wine about unions and co-operatives. The Finnish blueberry growers did something about it.

Old World Finland provided a long heritage of mutual aid and collective effort. The hard and sometimes oppressive poverty the immigrant knew in Finland fired among the settlers a spirit hostile to unrestrained acquisition of wealth. The difficulties of adjustment, the periodic unemployment and the general industrial unrest further developed the spirit of *yhteishyva*, the Finn word for the common good.

The co-operatives which sprang up in Maine were inspired by the flourishing co-ops in Fitchburg and Maynard, Massachusetts. Later, the Finns who took up poultry farming in the region of Union, Maine, established co-operatives, buying their grain and feed through these Massachusetts co-ops.

This co-operative practice was at first viewed with suspicion by some members of the native Yankee society. Yankees have a traditional reluctance to hang together for either good purposes or bad. To the rugged Yankee individualists, the co-op smacked of socialism. But when it became clear that selling blueberries co-operatively meant a better price for the crop, the Maine Yankee went into the movement with both feet and, in the case of the West Rockport growers, assumed leadership roles in the local co-op.

The Maine Yankee felt a basic affinity for the Finn, a fact that might well explain their ready acceptance of these North European people. Initial suspicion quickly gave way to grudging admiration, since the immigrant Finns possessed the same character traits the Maine Yankee honors and prides himself on possessing.

When a Maine Yankee testifies that the Finns are honest, hard-working, self-reliant, independent and a bit stubborn, he might well be talking about a Maine Yankee.

The role of the immigrant Finn in Maine's Big Woods deserves more than a footnote in the history of the state's lumber industry. It's unlikely that much wood would have been cut had it not been for the woods-wise Finns. The period of the Finn lumberjack in Maine was relatively brief—roughly from 1915 until the Depression years—but man for man, there were few that could match him with ax and saw.

There appears to be no reliable figure on the number of Finns in the Maine woods during this period, but if old-timers' memories serve, a good half of the work force was Finnish, and some camps were peopled almost entirely by these North Europeans.

The Finns who piled into the Maine woods in the course of this brief period were young, unattached and tough as boot leather. During the World War I manpower shortage, Great Northern and other Maine timberland companies set up employment offices in Boston in an attempt to fill their quotas.

The timberland owners couldn't afford to be fussy, but they knew they couldn't go far wrong if they overloaded their recruitment with strong-backed Finns. After all, whatever else a Finn was in the Old Country, he was no stranger to a saw and an ax. (Reputedly, it was the Finn colonists in Delaware who taught the settlers to build log cabins by laying logs horizontally rather than vertically, stockade fashion.) So the Finns were gathered up all over New England, piled into railway cars and shipped to Maine at the operator's expense.

Many of the settled Finns in Maine headed for the Big Woods as well in those years. If the quarries at Long Cove closed down, as they usually did in the winter, some of the unattached males took to the woods, to return when the quarries opened up again in the spring.

Leon White, of Bangor, for forty years a supervisor of camp clerks for Great Northern, believes there were never better woodsmen in Maine than the Finns. "They were fine people and honest. They gave you a fair cord of wood. When a Finn piled his cord, the scaler didn't have to go around back of that pile to see if the cutter was trying to get away with something.

"And they were clean. Many of the native Yankee woodsmen didn't take off their clothes all winter. The first thing the Finns did was build a steam bath. They bathed every Sunday, and after the steam they jumped into the lake, even if it meant cutting a hole in the ice."

The native woodsmen were far from unanimous in an appreciation of these foreign recruits. Matter of fact, they didn't cotton to the Swedes, Poles or the French Canadians when they first appeared on the scene. As one Yankee logger is reported to have said to his woods boss, "Me and the boys here can cut all the logs you want . . . you don't need none of them furrin' bastids around."

And the Yankee logger wasn't inclined to discriminate. To him, all the Northern and Middle Europeans were lumped together under the portmanteau designation "Polark." Some of the more perceptive native lumberjacks managed a bit more ethnic accuracy: they referred to Finns as Swedes, Russians, or squarcheads.

But it didn't take the Finn woodsmen long to gain a grudging respect from their Yankee fellows. Not only were the Finns good woodsmen, they demonstrated that they could "go the route"; that is to say, they stuck it out until spring. Few Finns legged it out in midwinter to "get their teeth fixed," the logger's euphemism for going to town for a bender.

Leon White recalls that the Finns stayed pretty much with their own, eating together and sleeping side by side. "They were quiet, sort of drawn into their shells. They did their job and did it well. While most of the Yankee loggers might sit around the bunkhouse after supper yarning, the Finns would be in the dingle filing their saws for morning."

While the Finn lumberjack couldn't be faulted as a cutter and piler of pulpwood, he was generally passed over for a part in the spring log drive. It would seem that Finns had neither the talent nor the inclination to put on calk-boots to shepherd logs down a river. As one woods boss said, bluntly, "The 'Polark' that can walk a running log hasn't been born yet."

Perhaps the Finns lacked a flair for the dramatic and, being practical men, saw little profit in competing with the flamboyant Yankee rivermen for a place in the body of lumbering legend; but for the best part of two decades the job they did in the Maine woods, they did quietly and superlatively well. By the mid-thirties the Finns were gone from the Big Woods of Maine, making way for the French Canadian. They left behind them an enduring example of industry, hardihood and probity.

It would seem that the immigrant Finns found in Maine an image of their own austere land. And the people of Maine found in the Finns a love of the land and a passion for independence they themselves knew and respected.

Perhaps only in northern New England does there remain evidence of how it was. Huddled at the crossroads stood the school, the church, the store . . . together they served the simple needs of a simpler day.

Like the Passion Play or the classic Western movie, the Maine town meeting is essentially a reenactment . . . the actors change but the roles are timeless.

Maine people have a passion for local autonomy and are jealous of the right to govern themselves as they see fit.

The last stronghold of democracy it may be . . .

. . . yet no sensible State-of-Mainer would encourage this pompous notion for fear he'd be obliged to wear a necktie.

In the one-room school students learned pretty much at their own speed. "The pupil paid no attention to the class below his own level but followed everything above his level thirstily. Knowledge was made to seem a lofty reality, vastly remote, yet priceless. . . ."

''. . . The one-room school conveyed a feeling that learning was better than other things.''

Ruohomaa relatives in Finland. The broad face, square jaw, blue eyes betray the ancestry of the Maine Finn.

When the land was cleared, sunlight released the blueberries. . . . This was a crop that required whole families in dawn-to-dusk labor in the fields.

They had a passion for independence and a love of the land. They worked together and came together in peace in the end.

THE SEA, THE SHIPS, THE RUNNING TIDES

Off to the Banks

The sea has exerted a deep and abiding influence upon the people of Maine. Shipbuilders, bluewater men, trawlermen, lobstermen, clamdiggers, all are a part of the sea experience which has shaped the minds and lives of generations of Maine coastal people.

The sea has made a few men rich and kept more poor; but whatever the material disparity, saltwater men have more in common with each other than with those whose lives and history are untouched by sea winds and running tides. Since men first dared to face its hazards, the sea has awed man and caused him to wonder. Its very vastness has brought to him an acute awareness of his small place in the scheme of things.

Man is a terrestrial creature: at sea he is a stranger. Through the ages, the bluewater sailor viewed the sea as a minatory presence—remote, impersonal and mysterious. The long voyages under canvas evolved a special breed of men for whom the sea was a hard master and a symbol of man's dark nature and obscure destiny.

The sea is still vast and unforgiving, but the men who serve aboard modern merchantmen and tankers spend little time pondering imponderables. For them the sea is a place of work, and their lives are little different from that of their hard-hat brothers. Today, perhaps only the fisherman is a breed apart. Certainly the Maine offshore trawlermen have changed little over the centuries. Tough, stubborn and unshriven, the Maine trawlerman fishes because he is a fisherman: for him the sea is a calling and a commitment.

European fishermen were finding a bonanza in the Gulf of Maine and on the Grand Banks more than a half century before Columbus set forth from Genoa in 1492. Those early venturers were not seeking glory; outcasts of the English mercantile society, what they sought was fish for protein-hungry Europe and a share of the riches their harsh life produced. The riches were seldom realized, but fish they did catch—and in incredible numbers.

There is solid evidence that land-based fishing stations were set up on the Maine coast at Pemaquid, Monhegan and Damariscove islands as early as 1520. It made good sense. Instead of running back and forth across the ocean with fish, a standby crew could remain and devote the off-season to making barrels, drying the catches, repairing gear and carrying on a little trade with the Indians on the side.

These hardy fellows, dragooned from the seaports of West England, were not to the Queen's taste. They were men without women, hard-drinking, impious, and for the most part, illiterate. Sir Ferdinando Gorges, sometimes called the Father of Maine, found them to be "stubern fellows." Sir Ferdinando and his associates had been given the fishing monopoly in Maine waters by King James I. A tax was levied on fishing vessels at the rate of eighty-three cents a ton, an assessment the fishermen flatly refused to pay.

The typical fishing boat of the period was about two hundred tons and carried fifty or so men. Each member of the crew put in twenty shillings, and as has been the hallowed custom of fishermen, the complement "went on shares." The vessel took one third; the second third went for gear and supplies, including salt; the remaining third was divided among the crew.

In the last half of the seventeenth century when shore stations were well established, smaller boats or shallops were used. They carried four men as a rule: a master who steered, a midshipman, a foremastman and a shoreman, who acted as cook. The latter also attended to the catches, washing the fish and turning them on the flakes.

The great proportion of the catch was salted and dried. Some, called "corfish" (corned fish), were packed whole in brine. Mackerel and herring were sold in hogsheads to be used as bait or sold as food to West Indian slaves. The cod livers were tried for oil, or "traine," and made a valuable export.

First in value were the full-bodied, clear-fleshed fish. Of second value were the fish not so full-fleshed, or those salt-burned or spotted. A third variety was known as "dun" or dark fish and brought premium prices in the early eighteenth century. Mostly pollock were used. These were caught in the summer and cured on rocks without much salt. Their flavor was improved by placing them in dark places buried in marsh hay.

Though France and Portugal led the way to the Banks, the English caught up fast. By 1634, close to twenty thousand tars had been pressed into the Grand Banks fishery, which became the proving ground for the seamen who challenged the sea supremacy of Spain and broke the back of Spanish power forever by destroying the Spanish Armada.

After returning from his voyage to Maine in 1614, Captain John Smith was stirred by dreams of populating the region with English fishermen and capturing the rich and expanding fish markets of Europe. For a half century after the defeat of the Spanish Armada, the English did in fact all but monopolize the cod fishery. She was forced to give ground to the Yankee ports that had the advantage of proximity to the Banks. And the Yankees managed to hold their position as a major fishery nation until the Second World War.

Today, the once proud Yankee fishery has come upon sorry days. Refusal to change outmoded methods, lack of any real conservation measures, and failure of the federal government to help New England meet the challenge presented by modern foreign competition have brought a steady decline of an industry that was once second in the world.

Maine men go to the Banks in battered, obsolete vessels, manned by a small cadre of professionals, the crews eked out with whatever the waterfront offers. The complements may be made up of a few steady family men, but there are as well the unsteady ones who can't hold onto a shore job; and there are some who ship out because they find nothing but trouble ashore; for them fishing amounts to protective custody. And always there are a few out-and-out bums, the winos and rumdums who are not much good aboard or ashore. They get sites on a banker when a skipper must sail and can find nothing better to fill out the crew.

The sea has a way of gathering to her bosom the misfits and mavericks society finds difficult to assimilate. They answer the sea call because only at sea do they feel whole and a part of something larger than themselves. In this they are not so different from their fishing forebears.

Call her the *Ladybird*. She's a typical Maine Banks trawler, a rust-scaled, 110-foot vessel with thirty years of service under her belt and an antiquated engine in her bowels. Somewhere in that gray expanse of fog and sea she has just hit fish. The first tow has dumped six thousand pounds of fish on the deck. The skipper is on his second tow. From the wheelhouse he can see the fish being forked into the hold to be penned and iced.

The radio telephone cackles. It's a call for the *Ladybird*. Someone named Mike wants to know if the skipper has found any fish.

"A few," the *Ladybird*'s skipper tells him. "Jeesly poor fishing, Mike."

He's lying in his teeth, of course. A trawler skipper always lies when he's taking fish. Immemorially, Banks fishermen have been close-mouthed about where they are taking fish. This explains why Christopher Columbus was given credit for discovering America.

The *Ladybird* should be carrying nine men, but with fishing getting harder and fish getting scarcer, she carries six. The work is killing, but the cuts are larger that way. And that means everyone works on deck once the vessel is on the grounds, including the cook and the engineer.

It's fifty to sixty hours of steaming to the Banks from the Maine ports of Rockland and Portland. It's ramming through fog, snow or rain at a good ten knots, for time not fishing is wasted time. Except for tricks at the wheel, the crew lives in the sack. Like squirrels storing nuts for the winter, trawlermen store up sleep for the sleepless days ahead.

Somewhere off Cape Sable the Skipper makes a Loran fix and adjusts his course. "Put her on the Big E—due east," he tells the helmsman. The helmsman swings the big wheel and puts it in the beckets. They are on the Big E. The next morning they will be fishing.

Only the Skipper knows where he's planning to fish. He doesn't tell the crew, and they know better than to ask.

"The boys call the pilot house the 'knowledge box,' " the Skipper said. "If I find fish, everything is the finest kind and I'm a genius. If I don't, I'm a no-good, wore-out brine pecker."

The Skipper had made up his mind before departure. The decision may be based on hunch, but a hunch laced with the stuff of experience. The fishing spots in that vast gray seascape are not visible to the eyes. Nor do they appear on any map. Rabbit Ears. The Rocking Chair. The Stone Fence. These are trawlermen's names suggested by the topography of the bottom. Ninety fathoms down the Stone Fence looks like a stone fence. Foul bottom, they'll tell you. A good chance to rimwrack your nets. In trawlerman jargon, any foul-up is a rimwrack.

It could be a gray dawn on a glassy swell, or high noon with a big sea running when the Skipper calls for half speed. His depth finder tells him he's where he wants to be. His fishscope tells him the fish are there. Two sharp toots of the steam whistle cue the action. There's a scramble for boots and oilskins. In a matter of thirty seconds, the crew's on deck and men are at their stations. No elite gunnery crew could match the performance for speed and precision.

To a nonprofessional, a trawl net stowed inboard is no more than a confusion of twine, rollers, spacers and cables. Two ironbound doors—"otter boards"—hang from gallows frames on the starboard side of the vessel. To the accompaniment of rattling winches and barked commands the nets are muckled to the rail.

The doors are unhooked and go crashing into the sea. Towing wire begins running out—three hundred fathoms of it. At the Skipper's command, the towing wire is grappled inboard and made fast at the stern. The Skipper, who has been dashing about on the deck, is back at the wheel now. The vessel is driving ahead under the press of her screws. The *Ladybird* is fishing.

The otter trawl is a refinement of the old beam trawl, a rig that uses two heavy ironbound otter boards roped to the wings of the net. The doors are hung at such an angle that they are forced outward as the vessel tows and the wide mouth of the net opens. The top of the net is held up by floats, and weights hold it to the bottom. Rollers trundle the trawl along the bottom and, in theory at least, bounce the trawl over underwater snags and obstacles.

The theory is fine. In practice, there are few fishing days that are not punctuated by rimwracks. It's usually too late when the Skipper at the wheel feels that sickening drag which tells him his nets are hung up. If luck is with him, he may clear the trawl. More often than not, the net is hauled back with the wings in shreds or the belly of the net ripped open.

In that event, there is nothing to do but haul the nets inboard. The crew, to a man, sets to mending twine, sometimes through the night under deck lights.

As was the case in those early days, the Maine trawlerman fishes on shares. The usual arrangement is a 40/60 lay: the boat takes 40 per cent, the crew 60, with the Skipper getting an extra share. Out of the crew's share comes the fuel, ice, food and the lumper's unloading charges. A good trip of fish might pay off a fisherman's mortgage or add up to a down payment on a new car. But he'd be foolish to splurge, because the next trip could be a "broker"—a trip that doesn't cover basic expenses.

Even when fishing is good, the trawler fo'c'sle isn't the happiest place in the world. When fishing is poor, it's a morgue. Indeed, the bunks on a trawler are sometimes referred to as "coffins." Since sacktime is brief and unscheduled, the trawlerman sheds little more than his boots when he rolls in. A week of fog tends to bring out the full ripeness of fish-gurried clothes.

Each year, the Banks takes its toll of men and vessels. Fire at sea is an ever-present hazard. A collision in the fog with another fishing vessel is bad enough, but when a trawler is struck by an ocean greyhound logging twenty knots—and this happens at least once every few years—you don't have a chance.

"Mending twine in the winter with seas piling over the rail, that's the worst," the trawlerman said. "You can't wear gloves, naturally. It's really tough on them old trawlermen with stubs for fingers. Stubs pain like holy hell when they thaw out. I've seen men cry like babies. There's times when I'm winter fishing that I keep asking myself, 'What are you doing here, you numb bastard?' I never get a good answer."

A good trip of fish makes all the difference, of course. When a gibbous cod-end is swung inboard and the pucker string is broken, spilling a torrent of slithering fish upon the decks, all bitterness and misery are forgotten.

A full trip of fish for the *Ladybird* is two hundred thousand pounds. A good trip is anything over half of that. A week at sea usually sees the tail end of the food, fuel, and ice. A good trip or poor, the time comes when the Skipper in the wheelhouse gives the word.

"Put her on the Big W," he says to the helmsman. The vessel swings, the engines turn up. The trawler is headed for home.

Home for the trawlerman is any one of a number of things. For some, home is the sea. For others, there may be a house and a wife and some kids. Home, for many, is the waterfront and three days on the town.

"You know," the Skipper said, "any reasonably tough brine pecker can take two weeks at sea. But those three days ashore are something else again. It takes an awful tough son of a bitch to get through those three days ashore."

The winchman put it another way. "Sure, I get drunk. And sure, I blow all I've made in ten days at sea in a couple of days at the bars. After all, it's only money. And who the hell would take a site on a trawler dead sober?"

Maine Lobsterman

In a state where anachronisms flourish, the Maine lobsterman is utterly at home. The delayed time frame suits him and he is not beguiled by the allurements of the modern age. As a prime producer he is locked into our entrepreneurial society, yet stubbornly retains his sovereign identity. The Maine lobsterman, whatever else he may be, is his own man.

Like that other paradigm of early American individualism, the fur trapper, the lobsterman is a loner by nature and a gatherer by trade. Year after year, he harvests the sea on his solitary rounds, unburdened by the need to till or fertilize his ocean pastures. Security he neither asks for nor wishes, for its price is curtailment of freedom. Again like the fur trapper, it is the never knowing what his next trap will produce that lends spice to the daily gamble. Any Maine lobsterman will tell you that lobstering spoils a man for any other way of life.

First of all, there is the setting. Maine lobstering takes place in an arena of superlative beauty. Eons ago, the Maine coast sank. Valleys and river basins became long indented bays, and hillocks became islands. The drowned coast of

Maine is as ragged as a wild pony's mane. Ungroomed, pristine, the seaward face of this northerly region is characterized by headlands cloaked with dark stunted spruce and shod with bold granite bulwarks upon which the seas surge and pound. Tucked away are snug harbors and some just barely secure, where workboats bob at moorings, encircled on steep-rising ground by raffish arrays of white or weathered houses. It is a region where nature dominates, austere, somber and starkly beautiful.

Though, essentially, the lobsterman tends his strings much as did his grandfather, he has availed himself of certain boons of modern technology. The day of the sweet-lined sloop has vanished, and rare is the dainty "peapod" once the standby of inshore lobstermen. Gone too are the single-stroke "one-lungers" that could be heard for miles, coming and going.

The typically full-time Maine lobsterman runs a thirty- to forty-foot powerboat, some equipped with depth finders and virtually all carrying two-way radios. Hydraulic pothaulers have taken some of the bone labor from the job. Synthetic rot-resistant nylon is today in universal use for warps and potheads.

For all his predilection for working in solitude, the lobsterman is not an unsocial critter. The predawn of any Maine cove can sound like a zoo at feeding time as boats are revved up and their seabound owners shout back and forth across the water over the gabbling of radios turned up full blast.

The standard concept of the Maine lobsterman as a taciturn toiler of the sea is a myth. Lobstermen as a breed are as vocal a bunch as one is likely to find outside a ball park. Not only will he talk; he will argue, protest and state his personal views at the drop of a bait bag.

In keeping with his old-fashioned individualism, the lobsterman is of the opinion that there are too many laws and too much regulation. He has no use for "Big Brothers" and their disposition to monitor his activities. The interest of the Internal Revenue Service in his income he construes as harassment and acts accordingly. Indeed, the Maine IRS Director stated recently that the "degree of noncompliance we found among lobstermen was most disturbing."

For his part, the Maine lobsterman maintains that the federal tax men don't know the first thing about lobstering. One fisherman complained: "I deducted one thousand dollars for twine I used for trap heads. This fellow tried to tell me that twine is used for tying up packages and that I couldn't have tied up that many packages in a year."

Vocal though he may be, there are some things the lobsterman will not discuss. Most certainly he won't tell you how well he's doing. His response when the question is put to him directly is that he's "catching a few." Traditionally, the lobsterman's daily catch is classified information and he'll go to extreme means to keep the matter private.

The archetypal Texan may be disposed to exaggerate his affluence. The Maine lobsterman will take pains to minimize it. He would like you to believe that he lives on a bare subsistence level. He calls his traps "poverty boxes" and wears threadbare clothes to support the myth. If this is an expression of the natural Yankee dislike of ostentation, it is also an indisposition to encourage competition.

Historically, those who follow the sea have felt themselves to be exploited and discriminated against by a land-based society. Lobstermen are suspicious of bureaucrats in general and in particular of state biologists, who for decades have attempted to set up controls to govern their activity. Nor do they rely with unquestioning faith upon the weather bulletin issued by the federal forecasters. As he prepares to set out to haul, the Maine lobsterman listens to the morning radio report with one weather eye on the set of the sea and the cast of the sky.

The saying goes that men who do not fear the sea are victims of it. Certainly, the Maine lobsterman respects the sea, but his caution is more a reflection of concern for his boat than himself. Essentially, he is a fatalist: he will go when his number comes up. The fact that few lobstermen can swim manifests this fatalism. Of course, there is the very good point that in close-to-freezing water the swimmer and the nonswimmer alike have an equally minimal chance for survival.

So each morning he makes his judgment. He may leave his boat at her mooring and let his traps "set over" and devote the day to repairing gear, or he can free his bowline and head out. If he chooses to go, it will be at full throttle, for he wants to be back at his mooring before the wind freshens, as it is wont to do along the coast in the early afternoon.

Salt spray blinding his windshield, he hauls on his weather gear. Bait in a tub at his feet, lobster gauge and pegs set handy by, he peers around the windbreak seeking his first pot buoy.

Sighting his buoy colors, he throttles down and hooks up the buoy by the warp. The toggle buoy, commonly a whiskey bottle which serves to keep the warp from tangling around the trap, comes up first. He shoves the boat into neutral and makes a turn with the warp on the winchhead. The clattering winch takes up the slack. When the trap breaches, he swings it up on the washboard and flips open the trap door.

It wasn't too many years ago that one pound of lobster per trap was no more than fair fishing. Today, the lobsterman considers that sort of production "the finest kind." In any event, in a matter of a few seconds, the trash and obvious "shorts" are culled out. The lobster gauge, set at the Maine $3^3/_{16}$-inch carapace measure, is slapped over the backs of the lobsters of questionable size. The legal lobsters, or "keepers," are pegged in to immobilize their claws and tossed into a crate; the flapping "bugs" that don't make the measure are flung back into the sea. The idling engine thrums again and, like a spurred pony, the boat runs for another buoy.

There are no more than a few old-timers alive today who remember hauling under sail. Dear to their hearts was the weatherly little Friendship Sloop; and it is unlikely that there was a workboat before or since so ideally fitted for the times and the job it was called upon to perform.

Listen to Ben Barker, now in his nineties. "You'd be surprised how nice those sloops worked tending traps. I'd just luff up to a buoy and let the sheet go while I hauled and baited up. Then off I'd go again. Those boats were just as docile as a milk-wagon horse while you hauled. When it was time to run for home, they ran.''

Maine lobstermen still are partial to fast boats. The fellow who knows but one speed—wide open—is referred to a bit chidingly as a ''cowboy,'' but very few are disposed to dawdle on their rounds. Fast boats not only cut down on hauling time, they get the lobsterman quickly to a safe mooring should a sudden storm come up.

Like most men who are beholden to the sea, lobstermen have their superstitions. They see nothing but bad luck with a boat that sticks on the ways at its launching. Many haulers are convinced that traps have an inherent success factor—born losers and born winners.

Sherwood Cook of Mosquito Cove likes to tell this story about a trap called Gwen. ''I named it for my wife, and I told her whatever the trap produced was her spending money—mad money, you might call it. That doggone trap was a winner. I set it a dozen different places in the course of one summer. No matter what bottom it set on, that trap would outfish every other. Finally, I gave up and scrubbed the deal. It was cheaper to put her on an allowance.''

According to Maine law, anyone with a proper license may fish for lobsters in any waters under state jurisdiction. In practice, this right to fish is not so simple. Much as did the frontiersman, the Maine lobsterman lives by an unwritten code and he is not at all reluctant to enforce it in his own way.

A carpenter may become a carpenter by investing in a set of tools. Lobstermen view any newcomer as an interloper and treat him accordingly. And the fellow who proceeds without thought to traditional proscriptions is in trouble. If he moves into occupied territory or sets his traps too close to those of an established fisherman, he may be given the courtesy of a warning—typically, two half-hitches around one of his buoy spindles. If such a broad hint isn't enough, he might find his traps damaged. Repeated transgressions may bring the ultimate reprisal—offending traps may be cut off and rendered irretrievable.

The best asset the prospective lobsterman can have is a lobsterman father. If he has a lobsterman grandfather as well, all the better. Although lobstermen of a Maine cove seldom speak with one mind, they do tend to band together in a loose confederation when faced with competition. If a local high-school youngster wants to put out a few traps, his presence is usually suffered. And once out of school, he's not apt to find much resistance if he decides to become a full-timer.

An outsider isn't accorded the same tolerance, and an ''outsider'' in Maine is anyone living beyond the outskirts of town. Nor is a local adult who goes into lobstering as an avocation greeted with enthusiasm. It is the muttered conviction of the lobster establishment that such part-timers are taking unfair advantage by holding down two jobs and taking bread from the mouths of those who depend upon lobstering for a living. Also, there is the abiding suspicion that the fellow who puts out a few traps on the side is often using this as an excuse to be at sea so he can raid the traps of honest fishermen.

Extra-legal though it may be, the concept of territorial rights is honored in Maine waters. Over the years there have been squabbles over fishing rights, of course, and even a few "lobster wars," but considering the absence of any legal means of gaining proprietary rights in open waters, the wonder is that problems have been minimal. As one lobsterman put it, "How do you think a bunch of farmers would get along if they all planted potatoes in the same field?"

Indian families of the Penobscot tribe held exclusive rights to hunting territories which were passed on from generation to generation; but such rights were binding only so long as they were exercised. Once a territory was abandoned, it was open for others to claim. This usufruct principle is today a part of the Maine lobsterman's unwritten code. Ownership of an island traditionally gives the lobsterman fishing rights to the waters surrounding it, but only so long as he exercises that option.

And like the woodland Indian, the Maine lobsterman is inclined to husband his precious resource. There are some outlaws, of course, but the bulk of the full-time professionals, realizing it is in their own best interest, are reasonably scrupulous in returning shorts, oversized and "berried" breeders to the sea. And, like that rustler "varmint" of the Old West, the trap molester is given short shrift. No one who is caught in the act ever fishes again.

For all his self-sufficiency, the lobster-catcher does keep a weather eye out for his fellows. His version of the "buddy system" is largely a tacit acknowledgment of the sea's capriciousness and his own vulnerability. There was that recent day when an Owl's Head lobsterman failed to return to his mooring. To a man, the local fishermen turned out for the search. When the boat was found adrift with no one at the helm and death by drowning was ruled, boats remained in the cove and all hands attended the memorial service.

There is no such thing as a typical Maine lobsterman, and probably never has been. It can only be said that members of this seagoing guild have more in common with their fellows than they have with other sectors of coastal society. If nothing else, the imprint of hard days in wind, cold and sun betrays his sea calling. The changes wrought in recent decades in the transition from sail to power and from an economy of plenty to one of scarcity have done little to alter the essential character of this breed of survivors of an earlier America.

Some adjustments have not been easy. The fathers and grandfathers of today's lobstermen lived for the most part on the harbor shores. The rise in the value of shorefront property has driven all but a few from a view of the sea. And perhaps today's lobsterman is a bit more concerned about his future than was his father. More and more lobstermen are fishing for fewer and fewer lobsters, and the good prices for his catches are offset by the rising costs of fuel, boats, gear and bait.

There is little the individual lobsterman is able or willing to do about the bleak situation. More efficient fishing or more sophisticated marketing techniques would serve only to hasten the decline of the limited resource. He will agree—if grudgingly—to submit to increased license fees and accept controls of the number of traps he may fish; but yielding further to state and federal dictates would so compromise this independence as to render his traditional way of life unacceptable.

Each year in recent decades there is brave talk about a quiet revolution that would make order of the chaos and bring modern-day efficiency to the fishery. That day is still far off. The Maine lobsterman's basic character doesn't accommodate easily to the demands of the marketplace. His battle is not only against the sea, but he is at odds as well with a system that rewards bigness and conformity and penalizes all forms of independent and singular behavior.

It is inconceivable that the Maine lobsterman will renounce his anarchistic independence and settle for corporate security. More likely, he will continue to speak his mind and struggle along on his old course, guided by his own personal views of the inalienable rights of life, liberty and the pursuit of happiness.

Cove Fisherman

Rockport's Howard Kimball is a man for all seasons. He lobsters until December, sets his traps for crabs in the winter, and stops off the cove if and when the herring strike into the harbor in the spring and summer. Back a way, he maintained a fish weir off his home on the waterfront, but the repair costs were too high and the catches too small to make it worth his time. Now he keeps a dory containing a token piece of seine at a harbor mooring. This means the cove is his and his alone to stop off when herring move in from the open bay.

Like most cove fishermen, Howard lobsters alone. Stop-seining requires a crew that shares the work and the profits. Howard Kimball's four partners split any profits according to each man's investment in gear. Lobsters and crabs are Howard Kimball's bread and butter: a few good herring catches can put money in the bank and steak on the table.

"I'm just a little fellow in this business," he'll tell you. "The big operators use spotter planes. They can spot a body of fish from the air and communicate its location and movement to a ground crew who move in with boats and gear. I don't have a plane. I do what cove fishermen have done for a hundred years: I count on the gulls to tell me when the herring are in.

"I call my crew and we go out at night to see if the water is 'firing.' A body of fish can make the water flash like quicksilver. Then we use 'feeling poles.' We cruise at a slow pace, drawing the pole through the water. We can feel the fish vibrate against the pole. Once we're satisfied that enough fish are in and well up into the cove, we run out the stop twine from shore to shore and secure it. Then all we can do is hope we've got a good charge of herring stopped off and that the price is right."

A shoal of herring struck into Rockport Harbor one recent spring. When Howard saw the fish breaking and the gulls working he phoned his crew. They arrived before dawn. Quickly, outboard-powered skiffs ran the stop twine from shore to shore. The pocket seine was made fast against the stop twine. In the predawn, a time when the fish are most likely to be pressed up against the barrier, the pocket was raised, the herring pursed. The workboats then proceeded to take up the stop seine and pile it into dories. It was time for breakfast and a wait for the carrier.

It was late in the forenoon when the carrier *Pauline* prowed in from the outer harbor. Fifteen minutes later, pumps were sucking a quivering mass of silver fish into her hold. Not so many years ago, buckets hoisted by winches bailed herring into carrier holds. Now hoses suck fish from the pocket like a giant vacuum cleaner, mechanical scalers scale the fish, the scales going into baskets to be sold for use as pearl essence in the manufacture of nail polish. As the fish slither into the hold, a deck hand with a shovel salts down the catch. The count is kept on the hold by hogsheads, the ancient measure of seventeen and a half bushels.

The packers were crying for herring that spring. Five carriers appeared in the harbor hoping for a share of the catch. The first vessel called gets her hold filled; the others take any surplus in the order of their arrival. Three carriers went away empty that day.

Once under way, the laden *Pauline* made radio contact with her plant at Bath. ''We'll dock around three with five hundred bushels,'' he told the super. Shortly before three, the carrier was sighted from the dock. The plant whistle sounded, calling the crew of women packers from their kitchens. Within a few hours after the *Pauline* bowline was made fast, roughly five hundred 100-can cases were processed and ready for shipment.

''A fair catch,'' Howard Kimball said, as he sat down to a dinner of dandelion greens and boiled potatoes. ''Years ago, a man could make a living just stop-seining. Not any more. You got to do a little bit of everything just to stay alive.''

Clamdigger

The booted clamdigger straightened up and eased his back with his calloused hands. ''Like everything else, clamdigging's not what it used to be. Sure, the price is better. When I was a boy, I got a dollar-fifty a barrel. Now you can get twenty. But there's not the clams there once was. They've cleaned them up. Oh, you can still make a good dollar fishing a tide, but you got to work and you got to know what you're doing. Some come out on the flats with a hoe, a basket and a six-pack of beer. Don't call that clamdigging.

''Used to be a two-inch limit on clams. You threw the little ones back to grow up. Now the state men say it don't make any sense to do that. The little clams will die anyway. I don't hold to that for a minute. You rake the little clams back into the muck and they'll grow up all right. I've dug clams for thirty years, off and on. I move around a bit, but mostly I stay in my own territory. You go off to another flat and some leaky-booter comes in and cleans up the clams.

''Sure, clamdigging is hard work, particularly in the winter. You don't get rich, but it's a living if you're willing to work. And you're a free man, your own boss. You dig a tide and you come in and hang up your hoe and you're done for the day. Beats working in a mill.''

Friendship Sloop

When the tall ships vanished over the horizon, the great wooden shipyards, which were the sinews of coastal Maine's economy, died one by one. For nearly a full century after the last of the storied clipper ships slid down Maine ways, most boatshops carried on the ancient trade of shaping timbers for workboats and pleasure craft.

It was a tradition that began in 1607 when a London shipwright named Digby built the pinnace *Virginia* at the mouth of the Kennebec, the first vessel fashioned by an Englishman in the New World. Now, after more than three hundred and fifty years, the story of wooden boatbuilding winds down to a quiet end. One of the last of the great builders was Harvey Gamage. There were others who honored the final decades of timbered vessels, but in terms of sheer production and lasting fame the builders of the Friendship Sloop earned a special place in Maine's maritime history.

Of course, one can still start an argument around the Village of Friendship over the question of who indeed it was who fathered the weatherly little workboat that bears the village name.

There were the brothers Morse: Wilbur, Charles, Albion and Jonah. There were "those other Morses": Oliver, Cornelius and Edward. And not to be overlooked were the McLains and Carters of that Muscongus Bay village of Bremen. You could take your pick and be as right as the next man, for when you come right down to it the Friendship Sloop wasn't invented in any real sense at all: it evolved by trial and error, by-guess-and-by-gosh, to fill a need.

The fishermen themselves had no more than a rough idea of what they wanted. Basically, they wanted a lobster wheelbarrow and a vessel that would take them out and bring them home. Of course, they leaned toward a boat that was sturdy and one that would claw off a lee shore in a blow and turn sharply in close quarters. To further ask for a boat that would take rough water without too much fuss was like asking for an egg in one's beer.

So it might be said that the fishermen around Muscongus Bay, in those last decades before the new century, asked for quite a bit in a lobster boat. True, they didn't know exactly what they wanted until they saw it. Then there was no doubt that the little workboat that was to gather fame around the world as the Friendship Sloop was it.

It didn't happen overnight. In those days there was a simple answer in those coastal waters to that hoary question, "What do you do all winter?" The sensible thing to do once the traps were ashore was to spend the time "getting up a boat." Naturally, ideas were exchanged and fine points argued. It might be said that the Friendship Sloop was born of pride and necessity. One story has it that the local fishermen running their lobsters and fish into the Boston Market were getting the pants beat off them by a fleet of fast little Gloucester sloops and taking a second-best price as a consequence. Then one day some Muscongus boys spied one of the Portuguese sloops hauled up on the beach. It didn't take them long to pile ashore and have a good look at her undersides.

There was a good deal of midnight oil burned that next winter on Bremen. Wilbur Morse was just another fisherman on the Island in those days. He was born at Bremen, Long Island, in 1853, one of eleven children. DeMorse had been the family name when the original five brothers came to these shores from France before the Revolution to establish an Indian trading post. Wilbur was brought up at a time when a boy had to fish to eat. Wilbur fished. Quiet and something of a loner, he mixed some private thinking with his fishing.

In the winter of 1873, at the age of twenty-one, he decided to get into the swim and get up a boat for himself. A few spare notes in his handwriting tell the story. ''I wanted a boat to go lobstering the following spring. I walked to Jefferson, about twenty-one miles, to pick up lumber for the boat and rode back on the lumber to Broad Cove, Bremen, the next day. I built a nineteen-foot boat. Used boat for lobstering in the spring. Sold boat to Randal Simmons.''

The next year he wrote: ''Built a twenty-two foot boat. Went lobstering in the spring. Did not build a boat the following winter. That was the only winter I did not build a boat after I commenced.''

That, in brief, was the story of Wilbur Morse's life. Once the boys knew what they wanted and learned that Wilbur A. Morse could build them the boat to do the job and at a price that was right, they never let him go fishing again.

Will Morse to his dying day insisted that a Friendship Sloop was a sloop built in Friendship by Wilbur Morse. That is not the same as saying he invented the Friendship Sloop.

What he did, undeniably, was to make the little vessel world-famous. He gave the boat a name and, by sheer numbers, made it recognizable around the world. Moreover, he was the first boatbuilder in Maine to have a glimmering of the assembly-line-production idea that was to revolutionize not only boatbuilding but all American industry as the new century advanced.

Wilbur Morse was just another boatbuilder when in 1900 he moved from the Goose River section of Friendship to the harbor waterfront and built a house and shop. What he had in the way of assets was a tight and skillful crew, a pocketful of orders and this new idea.

Viewed in hindsight, the idea was simple enough. The economics of the situation dictated pretty much the price the fishermen could pay for the boat. A Morse sloop sold for around five hundred dollars ready to go, except for ballast. That figure was a constant. There wasn't much profit margin there. On the other hand, raising the price would price the boat out of the market. The fishermen would go on building their own boats.

But say he had orders for twenty boats. By grooving the operation, organizing his production methods and eliminating man-hour waste and material waste, he could reduce the unit cost. And hold the line on the price. He could afford to take a small per-unit profit if it could be multiplied twenty times. So with a minimum of twenty boats a year he could be in business.

What had got Wilbur into the bind in the first place was the natural Yankee disinclination to turn down work even when he had more orders than he could fill. Now he realized that if he geared up properly he could fill those orders and make everybody happy, and most particularly Wilbur Morse.

He was reconciled to the fact that he wouldn't be loved by a crew brought up in the old ways of getting up a boat. But then he had his brother Jonah, who was not only loved but respected. Jonah became the shop foreman and eventually a partner. Jonah became the "working" Morse, and Wilbur the "thinking" Morse. Without this ideal tandem the new idea would never have worked.

Wilbur was quite right when he decided he wouldn't be the most popular man in the world. When he found his men talking he figured that talk slowed up his work. He had the gamming stopped. When he found a workman straightening out a nail he forthwith did a little figuring. Maybe it took only two minutes to make a usable nail out of the bent one, but if those two minutes were multiplied by a few thousand, that amounted to enough man hours to build a complete boat.

Will Morse was Yankee enough himself to realize that he couldn't restrain his men from this temptation to whack a nail into shape. What he did was assign a man to collect every bent nail in the shop each night. The nails were rowed out to sea and dumped overboard.

There were other ways to save money, and Will didn't miss many. He never invested in a set of lines. His favorite model was the *Nellie F. Parsons*, which he'd built in 1879 for a local fisherman who wanted a fast lobster smack. Will whittled out a half model. He sanded it down, and then, closing his eyes, felt along the hull with his fingertips. He always said that his fingers could find "bunches" when his eyes could be fooled. His fisherman customer, Herb Parsons, seemed satisfied, but Will continued to run his fingers along the hull shape.

"I tell ye, Herb," he said finally, "let's hollow out the bow a mite more. Seems to me she'll make less fuss in the water that way."

Will Morse must have got pretty much what he wanted in the *Nellie F. Parsons*, for he built more sloops off those lines than any other, a hundred or more. But that didn't mean that a fisherman got a stock boat. No one ever found any two of Will's boats alike. It's unlikely that anyone ever will. Will aimed to please. Say a fisherman liked the *Nellie F. Parsons* well enough but wanted a twenty-eight-footer instead of a thirty-eight-footer. Will merely made a scale rule to the size boat he wanted and went to work, adjusting the molds as the boat grew. No one but Will Morse was confident that the boat would come out right. It always did.

Despite all his fiddling, Will seldom departed from his rule of thumb when establishing the relationship of hull and mast. His strict rule was that the mast should equal the length of the hull and stepped back one fifth the length of the vessel from the bow.

It didn't take Will Morse long to set up his production line once he was installed in his new quarters. Pine planking came from Whitefield and was hauled from there to

Wiscasset by narrow-gauge railway and then loaded on a scow and delivered at Friendship at two-and-a-half cents per board foot. The keels were usually beech, and the timbers oak. The oak came from North Warren by ox team. Jonah Morse personally cut all the stems, keels and sternposts, using an adz and broadax, and with those ancient tools he had few peers.

The first boats were built at the harbor without power. Will quickly "modernized" his operation by investing in a steam engine to power a bandsaw and a planer. He got running water too. This was achieved by pumping water into the house up the hill to be fed by gravity to the shop below.

There were no lights, and it was this lack that brought about Will Morse's first confrontation with the bitter fruits of his new technology. His skilled crew of around a dozen men got two dollars a day for a ten-hour day. With the coming of the short winter days, Will decided to cut the workday to nine hours and reduce the pay accordingly. Their slimmed-down paychecks set the crew to muttering. The men were willing enough to work nine hours. But they demanded the ten-hour-a-day pay. The men realized that Will needed them as much as they needed Will. They also knew that with their tight production schedule Will couldn't afford the time to hire new men and train them to his methods. When the men threatened to strike unless he met their terms, there was little Will could do but try to mediate the differences. With the help of brother Jonah, he got the men to agree to work for the old wage until the current contracts were fulfilled, at which time they would get their raise.

It wasn't long after the wage fuss that Will Morse plugged up that hole in his production system. The day the steam engine blew up and sent the piston through the roof hastened the decision. The steam engine was replaced by a gasoline engine. A new generator was installed for more power tools and more lights for the short winter days.

At the height of Will Morse's activity he was launching an average of two boats a month, and there were as many as five boats a-building at once. It was often said, usually by way of denigration, that the Friendship Sloop was a "price boat," built for a job and at a price the fisherman could pay. To deny the fact would be to miss the point that it was this primary consideration of function and price that made for the simple and classic beauty of these sturdy little workboats.

Will Morse not only built sloops for a price, he built them for just about any price. The fellow got just what he paid for, no more, no less. If some of Will's sloops were underfastened or thinly timbered, it was because there were some fishermen who couldn't or wouldn't pay for a better job.

Will Morse had a good charge of pride for all of that. He insisted that his sloops were the fastest boats of their size in the bay. When his brother Charles, who had gone to Thomaston to build competitive sloops, took issue on this point, Will arranged a race from Thomaston to Friendship. Will beat him handily, by a full seven minutes. Nor was he reluctant to advertise the fact.

There were certain other situations where Wilbur found discretion the better part of promotion. During Prohibition days, some of the lobstermen who were using Will's sloops for smacking discovered there was a dead area next to the well that was not apparent to a casual viewer. No one knows how many of Will's sloops made a tidy profit running rum along with lobsters. There are no records of just how many final boat payments Will gambled for a percentage of the rum take. Old-timers insist there were quite a few.

The development of the gasoline engine saw the end of the usefulness of the Friendship Sloop. Will went with the trend and built powerboats for a spell. The time had not yet arrived for this sturdy, clipper-bowed little workboat to be called back by the sentimentalists to once again gladden the eye.

Will Morse, if he were alive, would be pleased by the staying power of the boat he made famous, if only because he'd be back at the same old stand. Sentiment would be a small part of his pleasure. It was in 1945, a few years before his death, that Carlton Simmons built a Friendship and named it in his honor. Will stood on the point below his house and watched the newly launched sloop, *Will Morse*, sail by. Later that day, Carlton got word that the old man wanted to see him. Over he went, expecting perhaps some grateful and sentimental words from the master.

"Boy," Wilbur said, "she needs more ballast." That was all Will had to say. And he was right, of course. She did.

Coasting Skipper

One September afternoon two decades ago, a spare old man slung a seabag over his shoulder and made his way slowly up the steep gangplank. Deer Islander Captain Montaford Haskell was saying goodbye to the coasting schooner *Mercantile*. The vessel was all but the last of her kind, and Captain Monty was the last of a breed that had for the best part of a century skippered these beamy little windjammers in the coastal trade.

Actually, the coasting era had closed after World War I with the advent of freight trucks and hardtop roads. As the coastwide trade languished, the tired old luggers were tied up at wharves to rot. It was Captain Frank Swift of Camden who came up with the idea of summer windjammer cruises for romantic city vacationers. A chosen few of these old luggers were refitted and called into service, along with Captain Monty Haskell. Now at ninety, with a life at sea behind him, the old salt was calling it quits.

On the dock, he made a seat of his seabag and gazed seaward. "I made my first trip on a coaster in 1880, when I was six, with my father, Captain Charles Haskell. I had my first command when I was eighteen. We carried all the trade there was from Boston to the Maritimes and as far south as the West Indies. There were few gunkholes those little vessels couldn't get in and out of.

''Ye had to know a thing or two to be a shoal-water sailor. No part of the bay that wasn't foul ground in snow or fog. Many's the time I've come through the Reach agoin' by ear. You make your course and let her come, with one ear for the bell buoys, the other for sound of seas on reefs. In a dungeon o' fog it's mighty thick pokin'. Never a vessel for speed and no great shakes to windward; but with a fair wind astern they could boil along at twelve, fifteen knots. In a following wind with all canvas drawing, you didn't have many vessels chawin' away at your weather quarter.

''You speak of hurricanes. I been through ten of them, more or less. One I recall especial. I was on the *George H. Ames*. We unloaded six hundred thirty tons of coal at Bermuda and were headed light for Jacksonville to take on a cargo of lumber. The gale hit us off St. Augustine. I ran her west for a spell headed into it, but she wouldn't right at all in that blow. So we went about with the wind under forestays'il. We made eight hundred thirty miles in three days, the rail ten feet under. If that wind had lasted a few hours longer, we'd a ended up ten miles into the woods. In that trade, if you weren't born tough, you had to learn how to be fast. You just never knew from trip to trip what kind of cussed lubbers you'd have up forward. The pay was low and the food nothin' extry. They'd come and they'd go and there was trouble both ways.

''This thumb now. That's another story. I kept myself in pretty fair shape in those days. I figgered I wouldn't al'ays be the biggest, so I had to make up for it with a trick or two and some fancy trimmin's. I was going mate at the time. There was a Scotia Bluenose aboard, a big loudmouth from St. Stephen. He'd licked every man forward, but that wasn't enough for him. This day he comes swaggerin' aft in nail-shod boots right across a varnished deck. I was there awaitin'. 'Go forward,' I said, 'and git yerself a hammer, and take every blasted nail outa them boots.' And he says to me, 'Matey, I won't take no nails out of no boots for any son of a bitch.' Well, he *did* take them nails out. It was two months afore I could get my hands in my pockets, they was that swole up.''

Before the turn of the century, coastwise trade covered a variety of activities, and these shoal schooners were built for the specific needs of each enterprise. In the span of years between 1820 and 1880 an insatiable demand arose for small schooners in the lumber trade out of Calais, Machias, Ellsworth and Bangor. In Down East river ports, where tides had a variance of twenty-five feet or more, small centerboard vessels could be beached at low water without damage. Long lumber was loaded through ports cut in the bow. A vessel with this unsinkable cargo was often so laden that on an even keel the deck was awash amidships.

The coasters wrote another chapter in the lime trade, and a perilous story it was. The slightest leak spelled catastrophe, for lime slaked with water could mean fire that could be suppressed only by sealing the holds airtight. The ice trade became one of Maine's important industries after the Civil War. Here again the little centerboard vessels played a leading role, for they could be grounded out on cribbing, and ice chuted into their holds from icehouses on the shore.

The coasting schooners spent their dying days in the granite trade. It was commonly assumed that when a vessel got too old for even lumber coasting or carrying wood for the lime kilns, she was considered none too antiquated for the stone business. In 1910, Captain Monty was involved in one of the last of the great stone-shipping enterprises in the Maine granite area. Going mate under his father in the Belfast-built *Susan N. Pickering,* Monty made twenty-one trips out of Stonington to Brooklyn in one summer carrying paving blocks for the streets of that city. Twelve thousand tons of granite were unloaded under what was then the new marvel of the age, the Brooklyn Bridge. Then the glory days of the coasters were over, but for several decades more the sturdy little vessels were common sights slogging along the Maine coast. They plied the coastal waters carrying freight into the coves and "eelruns." They stocked the tidewater general stores and carried coal and food into the fishing villages cut off from the rest of the world by snow and ice.

Captain Monty recalled the last load of coal he brought into the coastal town of Camden. It took a high order of seamanship to bring a vessel into a narrow harbor under full sail, and that was the way Monty wanted to do it that day. The deck hands stood by at the sheets and halyards waiting for orders to take off canvas. Not until the skipper was fifty yards from the coal wharf did he give the order—and then only to drop the tops'il halyard. As the schooner came boiling up to the wharf, Monty hailed a lad who was standing idly on the dock. "Take a line, boy!" Monty bellowed, "and if ye make it fast you've earned ten dollars." The lad caught the flying line and laid a pair of hitches over the bitt. Sparks flew as the line snubbed up and held. Only then did the skipper give the order to drop the fore and mains'il.

"In five minutes we were bagging out coal," the skipper said, a glint of pride in his dimming blue eyes. "That's the way we had to do things in those days to make a dollar."

The age of plastics has all but finished the craft of wood boatbuilding. A few small yards continue to fashion hulls with pine, spruce, oak and cedar. And so long as there are buyers who will pay the price for a custom boat, the diehard wood builders will struggle along. The old hands find the new material unloving to work, and a fiberglass boat unrewarding to create. The transition from an ambience of shavings to polyesters is too wrenching to suffer.

The tradition dies hard. "If God wanted man to build boats out of fiberglass he would have made fiberglass trees," says Chet Rittall, as he stubbornly carries on his small boatshop. But it is unlikely that Yankee pride and Yankee stubbornness will turn back the clock.

Sonny Hodgdon of Boothbay, who comes from a long line of wood boatbuilders, wryly considers his own uneasy future. "Sure, there'll always be a few wooden boats built for rich eccentrics who can afford it. A fellow may have to ask around awhile until he's told, 'Sure, there's still that old fart in Boothbay who can build one for you.'"

The Maine Grand Banks trawlerman has changed little over the centuries. . . .

. . . Tough, stubborn, unshriven . . .

. . . he fishes because he's a fisherman. . . .

. . . For him fishing is a calling and a life commitment.

It is the not knowing what the next trap will produce that lends spice to the daily gamble.

The lobsterman, whatever else he may be, is his own man. In a state where anachronisms flourish, the Maine lobsterman is utterly at home.

He'll tell you that lobstering spoils a man for any other way of life.

"The gulls tell me when the herring are in. . . . Years ago, a man could make a living just stop-seining. Not any more. You've got to do a little bit of everything just to stay alive."

TALL TIMBER, WILD RIVERS, THE SECRET PLACES

The North Woods

The question is sometimes asked why a state like Maine, so sparsely settled, poor, weak in all external aids, can send forth such throngs of masterful men, who, east and west, step to the front to lead, direct and do. We who were brought up among pine trees and granite know the secret . . . it is in the blood.''

Thus wrote Fannie Hardy Eckstrom in *The Penobscot Man,* her loving recollections of Maine rivermen and woodsmen. The past century knew the likes of John Ross, Billy Joe Savage, Larry Connors, Joe Attien—and masterful men they were by any measure. Legends are made by mythic men: the North Woods of Maine was the spawning ground of legends.

Big timber and wild rivers shaped a race of uncommon men. Loggers, woodsmen, trappers, hunters—together they wrote the rich and roisterous story of this other Maine, a region so different from the coast, yet alike in its harsh demands upon human endurance, resourcefulness and courage.

Taking up more than half the state, this vast wooded region is the habitat of the bear and moose and hunting cat; and eked out with a scattering of men without women who, gathered, would not fill a middling stadium. The Indian prized it as a hunting ground, the white man's lure was timber—first the virgin white pine, then the spruce, and now, for a half century, pulpwood to be rolled into paper which the world devours with little thought to the finite source from which it comes.

Like the sea, virgin forestland has had the power to stir men to awe. Wrote that early wilderness chronicler, John Springer: ''I was reared among the noble pines of Maine, nestled in the cradle beneath their giant forms . . . often I have been filled with awe as I gazed upon their massive trunks and raised my eyes to their cloud-swept tops . . . there are few who on entering a beautiful native forest would not experience delight.''

And of one personal encounter with a majestic white pine he wrote: ''I have worked in the forest . . . cut many hundreds of trees, and seen many thousands, but never have I found one larger than the one I felled on a little stream which entered into Jackson Lake. This was a pumpkin pine; its trunk was as straight and handsomely grown as a molded candle, and measured six feet in diameter four feet from the ground. It was about nine rods in length, one hundred forty-four feet, about sixty-five of which was free of limbs. The afternoon was beautiful; everything was calm, and to me the circumstances were deeply interesting. After chopping for an hour or so, the mighty giant, the growth of centuries, which had withstood hurricanes and raised itself in peerless majesty above all around, began to tremble under the strokes of a mere insect, as I might appear in comparison to it. It came down with a crash which seemed to shake hundreds of acres, while the loud echo rang through the forest, dying away among the distant hills.''

Springer's rhapsody ended with the comment that the giant pine was rotten at the butt; and the salvageable logs were too large to float in the spring drive and were left behind to rot.

In economic terms the tragedy appears to have been, not that the great pines were taken, but that they were, for the most part, taken too late. These islands of old-growth pine were overmature, dying at their crowns, hollow in their hearts; they had had their day.

Trees are as mortal as men: in the dynamic of nature, nothing is forever. Fulfilling the terms implied by the concept "forever wild" would be courting the hazards of fire, accepting the waste of rotting trees left by winds, disease and lightning strikes. Yet the alternative of calling the forest a "renewable resource" and relying upon management alone to plan its future would be to encourage use without accountability. Economics would decide what constitutes an "allowable cut," which in theory limits the annual harvest to the increment of annual growth, but in fact leaves the resource woefully vulnerable to the excessive demands of a wasteful culture.

Of all the human beings who have lived, fully one fourth are alive today, demanding to be fed, clothed and sheltered. Each Sunday edition of the New York *Times* requires one hundred fifty-three acres of trees. The paper sacks, napkins and paper cups used by the McDonald chain alone consume two hundred fifteen square miles of trees every year. In the face of such pressures, the Maine woods becomes a finite resource and a beleaguered island in an encroaching sea of humanity. In a brief decade changes in the Maine North Woods have been enormous and irreversible, and the transition from the old way to the new has only begun.

There is some validity in the corporate contention that the term "wildlands" is inaccurate as applied to their Maine holdings. The Wilderness Bill of 1964 stated that "wilderness, in contrast to those areas where man and his own works dominate the landscape, is hereby recognized as an area where earth and its community of life are untrammeled by man, where man is himself a visitor who does not remain."

Those Maine woods have been cut for two hundred years. Three or four generations of trees have been removed since the first settlements. Undeniable too is the corporate point that but for the continuity of the ownership of this major Maine resource and the discouragement of settlement, it is unlikely that today there would be any undeveloped wilds to preserve. Indeed, the Maine North Country has been trammeled by man, and man has returned and will continue to return. Today, timber roads, over six thousand miles of them, grid this forestland, cutting deeper and deeper into what was once sequestered backcountry.

Of the state's million-plus population, relatively few are personally familiar with this shaggy north territory, yet its very presence casts a long shadow upon the Maine consciousness. A legendary region, it is nonetheless a significant part of the image of Maine. There is pride in its presence, a pride scarred perhaps by a feeling of guilt for failure to share fully in the decision process upon which its future rests.

Certainly among the woodsmen, trappers, hunters and wilderness lovers there is the conviction that this wild domain is something more than a billion-dollar industry, infinitely more than a "tree farm" created solely for the purpose of supplying wood fiber to the world beyond Maine's borders. As the lovers wonder, men and machines continue the process of changing the face of what was once, despite the disclaimers, a wilderness.

It is doubtful if anyone will mark the instant when our wilderness is gone. There is a special poignancy in witnessing its demise, for there are few places left on earth where man can avoid his fellow men. Sadder still is the realization that such avoidance should constitute a special privilege and a blessing, and implicitly, an admission of man's inability to share the earth with grace and wisdom.

River Drive

It did not occur to Francis Healey that raw spring morning in the early 1960s that he was one of the last of a vanishing breed, that he was about to play a role in the final chapter of a long and rousing story. He had other and more pressing matters on his mind. A spare man in a slouch hat, he stood in front of the office shack at Canaan Dam and contemplated the cast of the predawn sky.

Boss River Driver Healey was about to close out the era of the long-log river drive. Pulpwood would continue to take the river road for another decade; then that too would come to an end. No longer does timber kite down a wild Maine river; nor will it ever again.

The cook's gut hammer sounded the call. The driving crew, shoulders hunched against the chilly wind, trooped out of the bunkhouse and into the cookshack. Some were young, most were grizzled, seasoned by a lifetime in the woods. They all looked rawhide tough.

They needed to be. For an indeterminate number of weeks, twelve hours a day without respite, they would be engaged in a job that would call upon all they could muster in the way of agility, bull strength and long-haul endurance.

For a century and a half the spring drive was the stirring climax to the lumbering year. Only the best were tapped to stay on to tackle the river. It was the ultimate honor to be chosen, and loggers lived by pride. The task called for the best in these best of men. Perhaps even more special than the riverjack "bubble-walkers" were the watermen who could take a boat down a full pitch of water. Then, at the very summit, stood the Boss River Driver, whose responsibility it was, and his alone, to bring the logs downriver to the booms.

On Oldstream that spring the man was Francis Healey. A million board feet of long-log pine was tiered behind the dam at the pond landing. Healey's job was to break the landing, water those logs, sluice them through the dam, and drive them thirty miles down a kinky little river.

Albert St. Pierre, Healey's French Canadian straw boss and a veteran of forty river drives, recognized a wicked river when he saw one. He was shaking his head as he joined Healey.

"Son-a-gun river for to drive, Francis."

The Boss River Driver permitted himself a smile. "Hell, driving logs is always trouble. The trouble with this river is mostly that I don't know where to expect the trouble."

Healey's uneasiness sprang from a realistic evaluation based on forty years' experience on Maine rivers. His guess was that this drive upcoming might very well offer something extra special in the way of a challenge.

For one thing, he had never driven Oldstream. In fact, there had been no drive of long-log pine on Oldstream in the memory of any living man. Peeled hemlock had run this river thirty-five years back. Pine, however, was something else again. Pine drives hard. It floats low, lodges easily and every tenth stick is apt to be a "bobber" or "sinker" bent on fouling up the flow of logs.

For two days the forces had been gathering. The wangan—food, gear, bedding—had come into the camp over mud-mired roads. John, the cook, had arrived the day before to get his cookshack in order. He needed more shelves, he needed more lard—and where in hell was his bread board?

And throughout that penultimate day the men who had been chosen to make up the crew had trickled in, packs on their backs. You could spot the seasoned river pigs. They walked with that rolling spring-kneed stride, the cuffs of their woolen pants bloused over their boots and held snugly in place with jar rubbers.

The buildup had continued throughout the day. By dark, tons of food had been stowed; bedding dumped into the bunkhouse; axes, dynamite, and gasoline, checked in and stockpiled; and pickpoles and cant dogs stood stacked and bristling against the sky.

Healey and the Frenchman strode down the slope to the dam. The impounded water behind the dam lapped at the eleven-foot marker. This, once the sluice gate was raised, was Healey's head of water.

The success of any river drive depends upon the Boss River Driver's control of the available water. That morning Healey was aware of his responsibility. Too much water and the flowage would carry his logs into the woods and meadows; too little water, the logs would hang up and plug the river. Run out of water? Healey didn't like to think of that possibility. If the water was used up before the logs reached the downriver booms, they would remain in the river until the following spring.

Francis Healey lighted up his cigar. "Guess we're ready, Albert. We'll heist her in an hour."

No one had to be told his job as the moment to open the gate approached. The crane and 'dozer operators crossed over the dam to the log landings to man their respective monsters. The outboard-powered workboats, to be used to herd the watered logs to the sluiceway, began to snarl. Men were picked to man the sluicing booms and point the running logs through the opening and into the stream.

Hunk Hurlbert arrived. A veteran and one of Healey's key men, Hunk was dispatched downriver to clear the "sweepers"—any trees or branches winter storms had broken over the river. As, ax in hand, Hunk hopped into a canoe, Healey said: "I'm giving you a few minutes' start. I'm heisting in twenty minutes."

Healey, like a battle general preparing to attack, was working on a timetable now. He assigned downriver stations. In a matter of moments the station men, equipped with pickpoles, cant dogs, rope and dynamite, were on their way downriver. Singly or in pairs, they would take their stations at Grover's Pitch, Hayward Dam, Joe Hill Dam, Stinking Jam Rapids, Longfellow Pitch—the names of trouble spots other loggers in another century had left upon the river.

Across the pond the growling crane had already begun to muckle the ice-rimmed logs. Healey slid into the seat of his jeep and contacted Whitneyville on the two-way radio. He wanted the last water-level report from the dams in the Machias watershed. That done, he nodded at Albert. Together they headed for the dam.

It took eight men and a fifteen-foot timber to prize up the sluicegate. The impounded water burst through the sluiceway with a thundering roar.

Healey's drive had begun.

Who knows who first got the bright idea of flushing logs down a wilderness river on a head of water? Likely it was a case of necessity mothering invention. Only in recent decades have timber haul roads gridded the big woods of Maine. Rivers were the only highways until well into the present century.

There was glory in driving a river. The East Branch men considered themselves a cut over the West Branch men, and the Allagashers considered themselves better than either. Supplies went upriver to the camps in the fall, and logs went downriver in the spring. Either way, the task was monumental.

In theory, there is nothing too complicated about driving a river. The key to the operation is the dam behind which the water, built up by spring rains and melting snow, is held. The water flow is controlled by a sluicegate, fitted across a narrow breach in the dam. When you've got sufficient water stored behind the dam, the winter-cut logs, tiered on the bank of the pond behind the dam, are rolled into the water. The sluicegate is opened. The logs are flushed out of the pond and downriver on a head of water.

But you don't drive logs with a pencil and paper. In practice, a river drive is a gamble all the way. The success or failure of a log drive turns on a hundred caprices of wind and rain. And as it had for two hundred years, the drive on Oldstream called for tough and catty men armed with ancient tools, the pickpole and the cant dog. And most particularly it called for the knowledge, resourcefulness and good judgment of a single man—the Boss River Driver.

And as always, the first few hours were critical. Healey figured that, without rain, he had roughly two weeks of water stored. What he didn't know was how much water it would take to raise the water level on Oldstream sufficiently to run his logs. Nor did he know how his logs would take the rifflings or how they would wing in at the coves and turns. All this he would know soon enough.

"Maybe I'm getting too old for this job," Healey said. "I've been driving rivers for forty years. Each drive takes something out of you, kills you a little. Once you let your logs go, you're committed. You've figured things out the best you know how. There's nothing you can do but hope the hell you're somewheres near right."

Healey's plan was simple enough. Five miles below Canaan Dam the river went under the "Air Line," the sole major highway across the Machias wilderness. Below the Air Line, the drive would enter twenty miles of almost inaccessible wilds. Five miles below the Air Line, at Stinking Jam Rapids, Healey had strung a gallus boom that would hold the main body of logs until he could establish a new base. Just beyond that boom was the ugliest stretch on the river: five miles of pitches, white-water rifflings, twists and hairpin bends.

Healey would wait until the main body of logs was behind that boom before he'd open the barrier and start turning his logs over the pitches.

His ace in the hole was simply this: once his drive reached this point he could count on a fresh source of water. Just above the boom, Chain Lake Stream entered Oldstream. At First Chain Lake, water was being held behind a dam ready to be released when Healey needed it. Before turning his logs over the pitches at Stinking Jam, Healey would open the Chain Lake gate. His logs would start on the second leg of their water journey on a fresh head of water.

Healey's logs were a long way from Stinking Jam that first day. Cruising downstream, he broke out at Hunk Hurlbert's station. Hunk was at the brink of a wild boil of white water, struggling to lay in the wing with his cant dog.

The "wings" are the logs that fill in at the turns and coves and build out at the rims of the pitches. The wings function as fenders and sheer the stragglers into the main body of flowing logs. Nothing that works is touched.

"There must be trouble above," Hunk shouted above the thunder of tumbling water. "Haven't seen a log in half an hour."

Healey was gone, leaving a wreath of cigar smoke. He found the trouble two miles upriver at Grover's Pitch, Dick Kilton's station. Dick had been alone when the logs had begun to fetch up behind a midstream boulder. He'd jumped on a running log, hoping to reach the rock, but instead he'd made a hole in icy water. Luckily, a cruising runner had come along. Now a half-dozen men were struggling to pull the plug.

There wasn't much talk in the cookshack that night. The hungry, bone-weary crew used their mouths to attack the cook's bountiful board. There wasn't much more talk in the bunkhouse, later. The rough board shack was festooned with drying clothes, and the stoked ramdown stove brought out the full essence of sweat, wet wool and hot boot leather.

Healey looked a little grim when he stepped into the shack just before the light was doused. To conserve his precious water the sluicegate had been dropped at four that afternoon. Healey wanted a couple of men to turn out at 2 A.M. to give Albert a hand hoisting the gate.

Porter Kilton, one of the old-timers, took his pipe from his mouth. "Looks like we're going to have one hell of a lot of rear, Francis," Porter said.

"A lot of rear, Porter?" Healey grunted. "Hell, it looks like this whole damn drive is going to rear!"

"The Rear" in driving jargon, refers to the logs that lodge along the river, fill in the coves and turns and make up the wings. Around two-hundred-thousand board feet of pine had been sluiced into the river that day. It had *all* gone to rear. Not a single log had arrived at the Air Line Bridge, five miles below the dam.

A river drive divides fairly neatly into three parts. The first phase is the preparation, the mounting of the offensive. The second phase covers the watering and sluicing of the logs and getting the drive into the river. The final, the longest and most grueling phase is taking the rear—sacking the river. Sacking the river means mopping up, cleaning every stranded log out of the stream, out of the woods and meadows. To sack a river, you need plenty of water. Healey was beginning to worry about the two weeks' supply of water that was to take his drive to Stinking Jam.

That next day, another two-hundred-thousand board feet of pine was watered and sluiced. Watchers at the Air Line Bridge had begun to see logs that afternoon. They were running down at about the rate of one a minute.

"That's not good enough," Healey said. "What's going to rear should have gone to rear by now. All my wings should be laid in. The main body of logs should be kiting down the river."

The aphorism "A stitch in time saves nine" is a guiding law when logs are in the river. Little jams become big jams in a matter of minutes. That next day there were plugs all along those first ten miles of water. At Grover's Pitch the boulder that had caused the trouble the day before was dynamited. Just below the sluiceway, the wings had begun to build out into the stream. Healey took the crew off the pond to get out on the logs and lighten the wings.

By the fourth day, Healey realized that his schedule had been on the optimistic side. His timetable called for all logs to be watered by Saturday so that he could begin sacking the river on Sunday. The logs simply weren't being watered fast enough. Emergency action was indicated.

Charlie, the 'dozer operator, passed the word just before chow that night. "Okay, you bank beavers, it's all hands to the rolling tiers in the morning.

Four-hundred-thousand board feet of pine logs got to be watered and sluiced before the sun sets. Hell, it only *looks* impossible.''

The impossible was accomplished that next day as men, machines, boats joined forces. No one cheered as the last pine log went bucking through the sluiceway and into the river. That was only the end of phase two. Sacking the river, the most grueling job of all, was about to begin.

Here again, the battle analogy is strikingly apt. Taking up the rear is a mopping-up operation. It's picking the banks and hauling logs out of the alders; it's prizing out jillpokes—logs rammed at right angles into a bank. The flotilla that started downriver from the dam consisted of four scows, several work skiffs and a pair of canoes.

Taking up the rear is all water work. It's jumping from boat to logs, from logs to boat. An acceptable toll is paid in cuts, bruises, blisters and bone chills from wringing wet clothes. Unacceptable but ever-present was the danger of slipping into a boil of white water or getting sucked under a wing. This can mean a ''call across the long swamp''—there is no straightforward word for death in the riverjack's vocabulary.

Healey had figured it would take a week to carry the rear to the boom at Stinking Jam Rapids. This time he was right on the money. So far, so good. But now came the ticklish operation: those million board feet of pine had to be turned over the pitches and sent on down another twenty miles of river to the holding boom at the Machias River.

Like an army, a river drive can't outrun its logistical support. The camp at Canaan Dam was struck. Food, bedding, gasoline and driving gear were piled into boats and borne downriver to the new base camps at Stinking Jam and Bear Brook for the final push.

In line with his master plan, Healey radioed to have the gate raised at First Chain Lake. The gallus boom holding the logs was opened. On a fresh head of water, the job of turning the logs over the pitches began.

With the end in sight, the battered crew worked with regained vigor. Once the logs made it through those next five miles of wicked water, it was easy going on the way home. There was a weekend on the town coming up.

Then the worst thing that can happen once logs are in the river happened at Oldstream: Healey had prayed for a little rain to build up the water storage behind the dams. Healey got his rain. But it was a matter of too much, too late. Once the logs had been turned over the pitches above Stinking Jam Rapids, he had no control of his drive, nor could he control the water that poured into the lower river from Joe Hill Brook, Sam Hill Brook, Dan Hill Brook and the scores of little feeder rills that contributed to Oldstream's flow.

166

A little rain wouldn't have mattered much. What Healey got was a three-day torrent. The water rose in the already swollen river. The water flowed over the banks. It carried the logs with it into the woods, into the meadows and logans. When the rains stopped and the water fell, Healey's drive was in the woods.

If it was a bitter sight for the Boss River Driver, it was an insupportable sight to his crew. The men had been driving sixteen days without a break. That night at Bear Brook camp, where a score of wet and weary men were jam-packed into a camp built to accommodate six, there were some mutterings. There was talk of bushwhacking out to town, en masse, and finding solace in a bottle. The names of two of the Trinity were taken in vain with repetitive vehemence.

Albert St. Pierre, who had nurtured fond hopes of getting home to see his family in New Brunswick the next weekend, didn't say much, however. Nor did Healey. And if Healey heard the muttering, he took no notice of it. He ate his supper, lighted his cigar and walked alone down through the aisle of trees to the river.

Nor did Healey say a great deal when he returned a half hour later chewing a cold cigar butt. Albert was standing by the cookstove with the men, drinking tea from a tin cup.

Healey said softly, "You've been driving rivers for forty years, Albert. You ever lose a drive?"

The Frenchman, Albert, finished his tea. He wiped his mouth with the back of his hand, thoughtfully. Then he grinned. "I go on my first drive when I have thirteen year. Now I have forty year driving rivers. By jese, would I be your straw boss if I ever lost a drive?"

That was all the conversation there was. No one left the camp that night.

The crew hit the river the next morning. They took the rear at Stinking Jam and started rolling it up. Wings were broken, logans cleared, jillpokes prized free. The stranded logs, once mere inanimate sticks of wood, became endowed with satanic attributes, each bent on eluding and frustrating the driver's single-minded purpose.

The rear rolled up. But the logs once returned to the river didn't keep on running like sheep into shearing pens. Down they'd kite over the rocky pitches, making a sound like distant thunder, only to lodge and jam up again at the next bend.

It was at Longfellow Pitch that the worst jam occurred. And it was there that Healey came the closest to losing a man. Bob Lupin was out on a wing when the logs hauled suddenly. He tried to jump ashore, but he found his foot caught fast between two sticks of timber. It was a miracle of timing that saved him. As the glut of logs hit white water, they separated. Bob got ashore on the bubbles.

Four miles in three days, the rear traveled. When Healey wasn't in the middle of the action, he was cruising the river in his powered skiff attacking trouble singlehanded when and where he found it. His logs were moving now. They were kiting down over the last pitches in orderly file—ten, then twenty a minute, and into the smooth, deep-flowing water of that last stretch of river.

On the twentieth day the rear of the drive passed Bear Brook, and Francis Healey knew he had it made. The next morning the cook broke camp. Healey was in the lead boat that towed the laden wangan scows downriver. Relaxed, he relighted his cigar and shook his head.

"I'm getting too old for this sort of thing. A man should have the sense to know when he's had enough."

Healey had no way of knowing he would not again be called upon to drive long logs down a Maine river, but the thought that he was the sort of fool who never learned when he had had enough was what appeared to give him pleasure.

Woodlands Manager

"Economics finished the river drives," the woodlands manager said. "It simply became too costly. For one thing, hardwood doesn't float. We're dealing today with seventy-six species of trees. Only pine and spruce and fir can be floated practically. And then, the men who knew the trade of driving a river became fewer and fewer. And who in this generation wants to learn a trade for a few months' work in the spring?

"And then, there's the mill owner with maybe a million dollars tied up in logs. He's paying interest on that investment. He can't afford to wait months to get his logs from the landing to the mill. And of course there's the risk of losing a drive. I've seen many a log drive lost on Maine rivers in my time."

He stood on the bank of the Upper St. John, the river he loves above all others. He had been born and raised in the St. John Valley, a descendant of the pioneers who had settled there early in the last century. As head of the Seven Islands Land Company, which manages well over a million acres in Maine's North Woods, he is one of the very few natives in the position of power and leadership in the Maine woodlands industry. Yes, he has seen vast changes in his time; but he didn't fear them.

"I'm not nostalgic about the past," John Sinclair said that bitter November day. "The past wasn't all that good to me, or my father and grandfather. I went to work in the woods when I was sixteen because the family needed the little I could earn. This working from dawn to dark for a dollar a day, living in lice-ridden camps, the instability—there was nothing pleasant about it.

"I guess there's been more changes in the woods in my time than there were in a full century before it. When I was young the farmers in the valley went into the woods in the winter and came out in the spring to farm. The Depression and then the war changed all that. The farms failed. The young people went away to find work. We skipped at least one generation of Maine men in the woods. Their fathers told them there was a better way to make a living; they didn't want their sons to go through what they'd gone through.

"Very little is the way it was when I first went into the woods. The horse is gone, the ax, the cant dog. Chainsaws, skidders, tractors, trucks, hydraulic loaders do the job today. The old family farm is gone or going. All over the state, marginal land is grown over and going back to growing trees.

"And more changes are coming. All over the world, people are looking around to find where the timber is and where the source of wood fiber will come from in the future. And they're looking at Maine. Because of increasing needs and the rising costs of transportation, mills and factories will have to be built right here in the state nearer to the stump. It could mean the stabilizing of the woodland industry, more and better jobs for more people.

"We'll have to learn to manage our forests better. We'll have to find markets for low-grade timber and for all species of trees. We need more vision, better planning and a better understanding in Maine of this valuable and complex resource. We haven't had a governor who truly understands the complexities that face us since Percival Baxter."

He gazed downriver and was thoughtful for a moment. The slush run had begun early that fall. The floating mass of mush ice made a soft sibilance as it slid by in the four-knot current. "There *is* something that I *am* uneasy about. The engineers will kill this wild river if they have their way. This river and six hundred million dollars' worth of timber will be flowed over if the Lincoln-Dickey dams are built. The government would pay for the trees and the land, the army engineers say. Those dams would destroy land capable of producing two hundred thousand cords of wood a year as far into the future as we can see. That land could mean forty million dollars a year to the Maine economy. We'd lose that and we'd lose this river, one of the few truly wild rivers left in America. They can never pay for that."

Outfitter

Lumberman, river driver, guide, Bert McBurnie has been a part of this country for most of his life, as was his father before him. He'd left the woods for a spell in the fifties. Now he was back.

"I vowed nothing was ever going to bring me back except in a box. But I came back. I guess it's true, you can take the boy out of the woods but you can't take the woods out of the boy.

"We're having a serious problem here with campers who just can't stop wrecking the camp sites. They feel entitled to wreck them, apparently, it's part of their vacation. When I was a kid there were a great many camps around here and they were kept open. We understood that if a camp were open it was all right to use it and leave it as we found it. There were three camps between here and the Chesuncook Dam twenty miles away. I remember a lot of times spending three days getting down. A head wind could make that lake impossible for a small boat. I can remember being windbound and forced to stay in one of these camps and I was glad they were there. I needed them. Those camps were important to us, a necessity, a method we had learned to help us live here. We had a personal interest in keeping them in good condition.

"Everytime you turn around people are stealing something. I have a canoe over in Duck Pond. I've always had it there, anybody is welcome to use it. Then somebody stole it. Some friends found the guy who took it and the canoe was returned. Today I was over there and somebody has used it and ripped about six holes in the canvas. I don't suppose it ever occurred to the people to repair the tears. Now I'm gonna have to hide that canoe in the woods and I don't like that.

"One time I towed thirteen canoes up the West Branch for a scouting party scheduled to come down the next day. I had six boys with me and we were all day getting the canoes up there. We got to Northeast Carry and went over to Lobster Lake to camp. We got our tents set up and I was really tired because we'd had to wade the canoes up a good part of the river. Just then along came some sports pretty well drunked up and started target shooting with .22s at tin cans. I didn't like that because I had the boys to be responsible for. I asked the shooters to please stop and I explained the situation. Well, they told me they'd do whatever they wanted to do in the wilderness and that it was just as much their campsite as it was mine. So we took down our tents and packed them in the canoes and moved to another site.

"I think it's great to feel we're going to leave this country to our grandchildren. So I have to tell a sport I'm guiding to throw his fish back. He says, 'Jeepers, what's the matter?' I say, 'You've got your limit. What do you want all these fish for?' He says, 'By God, I want 'em.'

"There's a change, a whole different attitude among those who are coming into this region today and it's affecting us, changing our way of life."

Logger

"The first winter I stayed in the lumber camp I was four years old. We were all Frenchmen in my father's camp. No Indians. I couldn't speak a word of English until I was about eighteen."

Vital Ouellette is an old man now. Now there is time to relax and time to remember. "When you went to a lumber camp you had to know how to use an ax. That's not so simple, but we had been raised with an ax. My brother and I learned from my father. By the time we were sixteen we could use an ax as well as any man.

"A lumberman knows how to cut a tree, knows where he is going to drop it. A tree three feet through you notch in front facing where you want it to fall. Then you cut it behind watching your corners. If the tree is not leaning the way you want it to fall, you put a wedge in the cut and hit it with a sledge hammer. Then you saw more and if you are a woodsman you know how much. Then pound the wedge some more and the tree comes down.

"When I first started with father we all slept under one great blanket that covered fifteen men side by side. If you were in the middle you just couldn't get out. If you were too cold or too warm there was nothing you could do about it. The food was rough, no sugar, no milk, no coffee, no eggs. No greens, no fruit. We had beans three times a day and salt pork boiled, pea soup once a week, boiled salted codfish once a week, boiled beef cut with an ax. It was frozen outdoors hung in a tree.

"When I grew to sixteen I hired myself to a lumber company and stayed in the camp five and a half months without coming out at all. Once into the camp we stayed there all winter. There would be fights. I saw some beautiful fights. If one man wanted to show he was a better man, they'd go outside and we'd form a circle around and let them fight until one man called enough. After the fight it was over, one man was better and it was settled.

"A woodsman had to know how to handle horses. There was one pair of horses for seven men. One man was teamster, three choppers, one sled tender, two swampers making roads. It's cold in that country and by January there are plenty of days forty below zero. Once in a great while we'd stay in because the foreman would be afraid for the horses—not the men.

"At forty below you shouldn't have horses in the woods. I saw a pair of horses freeze one time. They had come down with a big load of yellow birch logs. When those horses got to the landing, they were very warm, the steam rising from them in clouds. The snow was so cold the sled was pulling twice as hard, like pulling on sand. At ten or fifteen above zero a sled runs easy, but at thirty or forty below zero a sled pulls very hard. The teamster had to wait to get unloaded and right where he has to stop his team there was a wind making it maybe fifty below zero. By God, before he had time to care for his horses, unhook them and ride them or run them, they started to shake and down they went. They died right there. That was a terrible sight.

"How I started on my own, well I knew how to cut wood. The company furnished me the capital to get started and so I did: so much money a week for so many men. In the fall I'd pay them back. It wasn't too long that I didn't have to borrow and could work on my own. I've been going that way ever since.

"We got machines now and it's pretty tough for a small operator to buy them. A man now has got to have a good tractor to build his roads, a skidder to yard his wood, and a truck and loader to load and haul. A man can't make a living with just a truck hauling wood. Everything's against him. The man in the woods works cheaper than anybody, I'll tell you. Woodsmen will work twelve to fifteen hours a day, sometimes seven days a week, to make a living. But you don't hire a man and make him do that. I guess that's the difference between a woodsman and an employee."

Stranger

In the dusk of a February day in the early 1960s, a trapper named Armand Caron, returning to his line camp on a Maine wilderness lake, heard a strange cry. His first thought was that it might be a loon; but quickly decided there could be no loon on that frozen lake.

As he stopped to listen, the cry came again, a lonesome and rather melancholy wail, a sound he had never heard before.

The trapper's life is a lonely one. The voice of a fellow creature in a still white world is welcome. And so it was to Armand Caron until proceeding across the lake, he came upon tracks in the snow. He realized that a four-footed stranger had entered his domain. What he had heard on that northern lake was the song of the coyote.

Later he said, "It gave me sort of a chill. Always heard that coyotes were bad customers. I went on to my camp and got out my old Winchester; then I put it down again. Don't know why, but I did."

Armand Caron's initial reaction had been natural enough. From the time the American tide of empire had begun to push west, Don Coyote had had top billing on the settler's blacklists. He had been shot, trapped, clubbed and poisoned by the thousands. The coyote, *Canis latrans*, is of the wolf family of course—prairie wolf is another name for him—and for centuries children's literature has proclaimed the wolf a scoundrel. As the game warden said to Armand when he heard that the trapper had forborne to kill the coyote, "You're supposed to shoot coyotes, my friend."

For several decades prior to Caron's experience, there had been intimations that this shy and canny stranger had found a new home in the deep woods of northern New England. Newspapers carried reports of sightings by hunters and woodsmen of a wolflike animal; doglike tracks in the snow where no dog should be were stumbled upon. The stranger, by all accounts, was larger than a western coyote, yet somewhat smaller than a timber wolf.

Then, finally, one of these exotic creatures was shot by a deer hunter and strung up for public view. He had been termed variously a wolf, feral dog, coydog, coywolf. Once a thorough scientific examination had been made, all speculations were laid to rest. The stranger was officially identified as *Canis latrans*. The coyote had come to Maine.

The journey eastward had not been accomplished overnight. As early as 1910, coyotes were reported in upper New York State; twenty years later, in Vermont;

and then in the early 1960s, in New Hampshire. Reconstructing the coyote's creeping passage eastward, wildlife biologists theorized that the movement had stemmed from southern Ontario around 1900, the migration heralded by a buffer zone of hybridization—probably coyote-wolf crossings. By the time the first Maine coyote was available for examination, the wild canid was breeding true, producing offspring consistently uniform in appearance and traits.

In view of its size—one third again larger than the western coyote—the stranger first was tabbed the ''new wolf.'' Today the scientific consensus is that this new citizen of the American Northeast is a true coyote. This wise and durable canid, so long identified with the life and lore of the West, had succeeded in making an incredible journey against the tide of settlement. The coyote had extended his range despite man's malice and unrelenting efforts to eradicate him. He had come so quietly and had remained so unobtrusive that the truth of his presence amounted to a revelation.

The new immigrant was not greeted in his newfound home with unalloyed joy. He evoked the same groundless fears, recalled the same dark myths that have been the coyote's lot to engender throughout America's history. Americans are proud of their pioneer heritage. Our forebears were brave, resolute and resourceful. Strange it is that those early trailblazers did not recognize and admire like traits in the coyote.

Sympathy for wild animals was not a strong element in the early American tradition. The western Indians called Don Coyote ''God's Dog'' and revered him. The Indian's identification with his fellow creatures was an extension of his harmony with nature. The frontiersmen did not have or wish to take the time to cultivate this attitude of sharing the earth.

The unrelenting pressure on the coyote in his natural range in the West may have been a factor in his migration eastward. Certainly a contributing factor was the virtual extinction of the larger predator species in the East. The wolves had been wiped out by search-and-destroy missions shortly after the Civil War. Thus a niche was open to the coyote. Here in the East was a bounteous pantry, and the coyote, the most opportunistic of mammals, was nothing loath to fill the niche, fulfilling nature's aim of establishing an equilibrium in her domain.

Although similar in many ways, the coyote and wolf display distinctly different social behavior. Wolves have evolved into complex social animals and typically live in packs. Coyotes, on the other hand, are inclined to be loners. For them, two is company and three a crowd. There is some evidence that coyotes were not always so ungregarious. Quite obviously, the coyote learned soon enough that packs are more vulnerable to human depredation, and the selection process eventually produced a breed of recluses.

This antipathy for company does not extend to the family circle. Coyote parents are gentle and protective with their young and will remove pups to a safe location when threatened. Both parents contribute to the upbringing of the litter, and if one of a pair is killed, the mate will continue parental duties alone. Coyote litters average five or six pups, but in areas where coyote densities have been reduced below what the range can support, litters of ten or more have been observed. Coyotes appear determined to survive as a species.

Another reason for the coyote's success is his varied diet. Wolves tend to pursue and consume large prey species. The coyote lives primarily upon small mammals—rabbits and rodents constituting the major proportion of its diet. Only in late winter and early spring does the deer become a significant food source. The University of Maine's Henry Hilton in his recently completed study noted that many of the mature deer killed by coyotes showed signs of poor health, and all the coyote-killed fawns examined were smaller than average.

Unlike the wolf, the coyote is able to survive on insects and vegetation when no other food is available. And contrary to opinions expressed by some of Maine's coyote ill-wishers, Hilton found no evidence that beaver, grouse and songbirds comprise a significant portion of the coyote's diet.

Related to the coyote's adaptability is his incredible physical endurance. Tireless, he will travel up to a hundred miles over a period of months in search of food. A marvel of grace and agility, he can swim, leap and spring, all with the greatest of ease. Yet for all his physical prowess, the coyote's survival against long odds must be attributed largely to his superior intelligence. Maine trappers, who have come to accept the coyote as something more than a passing phenomenon in the Maine North Woods, testify to his canniness. Maine coyotes have been known to uncover every trap in an area and consume the bait without springing a single trap. And as is true in the West, the Maine coyote has begun to be extremely wary of poisoned animal carcasses set out to attract and undo him. Unwittingly, man may be turning the coyote away from its useful function of scavenging in favor of live prey he can trust as food.

Maine wildlife biologists and conservationists are all but unanimous in the opinion that predators do not exert an appreciable depressive influence upon prey species. Quite the contrary, all evidence suggests that predators in their own interests live on surpluses and that the presence of predators in a habitat is an indication that surpluses exist. Historically, it has been man's clumsy attempts to interfere with nature's balance which have destroyed a healthy equilibrium in the natural realm; yet here in the American Northeast a vocal coterie of outdoor writers and hunters call for the coyote's extirpation with vigilante passion.

The position of those who "cry varmint" is that the coyotes kill deer and that man can better perform the predator function of killing excess game. They do not wish to be reminded that wild predators are opportunistic hunters and that the weak and diseased are the most frequent victims of their forays, which results in a healthier prey species. The human hunter, on the other hand, is inclined to select specimens in prime condition, which inevitably degrades the herd.

Maine game-management men are inclined to the opinion that the establishment in the state of an effective predator will in the long run have a beneficial effect upon the Maine deer herd. The Maine Department of Inland Fisheries and Wildlife takes a wait-and-see position in the matter, but for the present at least there is small likelihood that a bounty will be placed upon the Maine coyote.

Admittedly, there exists in man an atavistic fear of creatures who deal death with claws, fangs and tearing beaks, and quiet reason is hard put to still that deep-residing unease. And there are those who see nature and man in an adversary relationship rather than one of accommodation.

Though the taxonomists have yet to agree on an official designation for the Maine coyote, there appears to be a general acceptance that the stranger is now stabilized as a genetic entity. The consensus is that this Maine canid is intermediate between wolves and western coyotes in nearly all respects and that the strain has purified to produce a coyote subspecies qualified to carry the designation Eastern Coyote, or perhaps *Canis latrans mainiacis*.

In any event, though no population figures are available, the Maine coyote has succeeded in this corner of the earth and is today well-established throughout the state. Nor is the continuing effort to blacklist him as a varmint likely to diminish his prosperity in his adopted home, for the resilient coyote has long since learned to deal with adversity and persecution.

And gratefully, the coyote has friends in Maine who welcome him; and those woods-wise ones who, if they do not welcome him, accept his presence with equanimity.

Joe Landry had spent the last twenty years of his life living alone in a shack by a backcountry lake. He stood with the game warden this March day looking down upon the remains of a small doe deer. The warden checked the pattern of coyote tracks and shook his head. Joe smiled. He himself had taken from the woods what he had needed to survive and no more than he had needed.

"Sure, coyotes kill deer, maybe even healthy ones if they can manage it," Joe said. "But y'know, Harry, when the good Lord created the earth, I figger he had other things in mind beside deer and even sinners like me."

Hunter

Perhaps only in the Deep South does there exist today a hunting tradition comparable to Maine's, a love and a lore that have been passed down from father to son uninterruptedly for generations.

In his scholarly tome *A Study of History*, Arnold Toynbee dismisses the state as a "relic of seventeenth-century New England, inhabited by woodsmen and watermen and hunters." The Maine hunter is inclined to accept this judgment with equanimity. If an anachronism he be, he wears the role comfortably.

Certainly, he feels no need to apologize for his pleasure in hunting. He will leave it to those who lack the deep roots in the tradition to defend the pursuit of wild game. For him, it is begging the question to argue that man is a violent species; that his tearing teeth and a gut capable of digesting animal flesh are proof enough of man's predatory heritage. The Maine man hunts because he has always hunted.

The rural boy takes the killing of his own meat as a part of life. The skinning of a rabbit is no more repugnant to him than the shucking of a peck of peas. Having never known guilt in the exercise of his hunting pleasure, he requires no absolution. The understanding of the ethos of the hunt is not so much acquired as instilled. It took three hundred years to make a Maine hunter.

From all accounts, the original Maine settlers were not expert hunters: they were yeomen, hewers of wood, sowers of corn. They had been bred in an English society where hunting was a privilege reserved for the high and the mighty, and the taking of wild game by commoners constituted the crime of poaching.

But those first immigrants learned the art of hunting quickly enough. Necessity dictated that they avail themselves of the bounty the wilds offered. And these frontiersmen had good teachers, perhaps the finest in the Western Hemisphere. Hunting ruled the life of the Maine woodland Indian: his society was structured by the hunt. The Abnaki tribes, because their survival depended upon it, refined the craft of hunting to an art.

Even after the white man's gun became available, the Maine Indian relied more upon good hunting than good shooting. It was the skills of still-hunting and the stalk, the arts which brought the hunter face to face with his quarry, upon which the brave prided himself. The Maine hunter has not forgotten his early lessons. He is today essentially an Indian hunter.

Modern technology has improved sporting arms to a point where man's advantage vis-à-vis the game may have shifted in favor of the hunter. The one-week-a-year hunter is inclined to avail himself of this increasingly sophisticated weaponry. Inevitably, as gun ranges increase and weapons become more efficient, the ancient skills deteriorate.

The native Maine hunter appears to have resisted this course. The old Model 94 Winchester, a good brush gun with an effective range of no more than one hundred yards, remains his favorite weapon. Like the Indian hunter, he prefers to succeed as a hunter rather than a shooter. Thus, he is able to gain that intimate relationship with the wild world that only hunting on the quarry's terms can provide.

Consider the Maine man in the context of the society in which he exists. He works hard—as indeed he must to survive in what, by national standards at least, is a poor state—yet steadfastly he refuses to compete for economic status at the cost of his freedom. His days are not structured by rigid patterns of work and pleasure. He does not, as it were, lead two lives: one consumed by obligatory occupation, the other the reward for this joyless effort.

So long as he agrees with them, the native hunter is inclined to play the game according to the rules. And for the most part, his personal code conforms to the legal statutes. However, he has no compunction about ignoring those laws he considers unfair or foolish.

In Maine, the term "poaching" is used in the broad sense of any game violation. The term in its ancient sense of trespass to hunt on private lands has little currency in the state. To gun on posted land may be a misdemeanor, but it is also a challenge. It is the grassroots conviction that the newcomer arrives in the state equipped with NO HUNTING signs, and the sooner he is put straight, the better. Maine judges tend to support the hunter's attitude in this matter, meting out fines for such violations at minimal levels.

The Maine hunter admits, if grudgingly, that game laws are necessary. He is quite aware that uncontrolled hunting and fishing would quickly bring an end to the harvest of nature's bounty as his forebears have known it. A traditionalist, he is concerned with perpetuation and willingly cooperates in stocking, banding and other game-management programs.

This does not mean that the native outdoorsman agrees with all management programs. There are almost as many opinions in such matters as there are hunters. The only discernible consensus among seasoned hunters who have spent a lifetime in the woods is that no "book-learned," fresh-out-of-college biologist possesses the qualifications to dictate game-management policy.

The Maine hunter is saddled with other stubborn prejudices. For one, he is chary of the word "sportsman." The word smacks of privilege, Abercrombie & Fitch clothes and trophy heads. The somewhat pejorative word "sport" underlines this suspicion. A sport, in regional parlance, is an out-of-stater who stays at sporting camps, hires a guide to shoot a deer for him, and gets lost in the woods the moment the guide turns his back. Such a judgment is patently unfair, but no more unjust than the out-of-stater's common notion that you need only scratch a native hunter to find a poacher.

Night hunting is viewed darkly by both Maine hunters and judges. Since no skills are called upon and the end is merely slaughter, the act of shooting game under a light has few defenders. This does not mean that the game warden can expect help in the conviction of night-riding practitioners. In Maine villages chances are good that the culprit is related by blood or marriage to half the town. Tribal loyalties run deep.

Though he sees the last of America's frontiers disappearing, the Maine hunting man is slow to acknowledge that his own wilderness is threatened as well. While he recognizes the need for restraint and forbearance, he is reluctant to accept what even the hunters of prehistory realized: that good hunting for everyone results in good hunting for no one. The Abnaki society was based upon privilege, the most powerful families holding the best hunting grounds. Commonly, the young brave married with an eye to gaining, through his squaw, access to more productive hunting territory. The storybook picture of the early American landscape teeming with game is false. Since man first set forth to hunt he has known cyclic periods of good and bad years, years of plenty and times when the spectre of starvation haunted his camps.

The native Maine hunter may be prepared to consider the notion that hunting should be a privilege rather than a right, but he would like to retain the final vote in any decision as to who the privileged shall be. If he is forced to relinquish a portion of his traditional rights, he will not willingly do so for the accommodation of those fellows from New York or New Jersey.

The Abnakis fought bitter wars with both the white man and the fearsome Iroquois over hunting grounds. Not so different is the spectacle today of the native hunter prepared to do battle against the invading hordes which each fall descend upon his traditional hunting territory. To him, the official argument that game management could not be funded without the money these visitors pour into the state coffers is not persuasive. The suspicion persists that the state bureaucracy is perpetuating itself at the native hunter's expense.

Undeniably, the Maine woods is feeling the effect of the endemic urge to get back to nature. In ever-increasing numbers, the passionate pilgrims are crowding Maine's woods, lakes and streams, seeking a sort of instant salvation from the ills of a materialistic American culture. Though man's survival no longer depends upon the hunt, the hunger to return, if only briefly, to the primal state from which man has so recently emerged persists deep in the inner folds of his being.

For his part, the Maine hunter has never wandered far from his biological roots. He has chosen to remain apart from the affluent American society. His riches derive from a sense of place, a familiarity with some bend in a river, his knowledge of a grouse cover on some upland meadow, or a rocky crown of a bleak mountain where the bobcat goes to ground.

For all his prejudices, the Maine gunning man is a lover of the secret places of the earth, a lover of the land. What he fears above all are the hordes outside his gates. His urge is to put off the day when all wildness will be trampled from the earth.

Moosetowner

In a region as vast as the Maine North Woods, change does not wield a new broom. Inevitably, there are holdouts, pockets of resistance, dust-mice of the past that have eluded or not yielded to the search-winds of change.

A fire sweeping across a bog will bypass hidden nooks too green or moist to feed the flames. A botanist discovers a forgotten species of snapdragon blooming on the banks of the Upper St. John River. A fly fisherman at the mouth of the Little Black strips in a rare golden trout. A decade ago, an eastern mountain lion that has not appeared on lists of Maine fauna since 1891 was sighted crossing a woods road at dusk. Sightings of these shy cats have been reported regularly ever since, leaving unanswered the question of whether the Big Cat has returned or had never departed his ancient home. And above the snaking Allagash, a few bald eagles soar, unaware that they are survivors of a vanishing race.

And consider the Moosetowner. A descendant of the English and Scotch-Irish pioneers who came upriver from the Maritimes early in the last century, the Moosetowner had managed to retain his distinct identity. The term ''Moosetowner,'' as applied to the citizens of Allagash Plantation by their neighbors in the valley, can be derisive or respectful; either way, the designation acknowledges the singularity of this small enclave that has survived intact and in place at a spot where the Allagash and St. John rivers meet.

This was moose country when those first settlers arrived. And moose country it remains; yet the likelihood is that this folk name derives not so much from the presence of this magnificent beast as from his character. The moose is unpredictable, disputatious and scornful of those who would challenge his right to his ancient domain.

Whether by heavenly fiat or adverse possession, the Moosetowner lays claim to the woods surrounding him and the game therein. Though this forestland for the most part is owned by large timberland companies, trespass cutting has been the Allagasher's way of life for generations. The Moosetowner, in consequence, is a thorn in the socks of the region's timberland owners, who at one period during the Depression discovered that the only way they could get needed timber was to buy back stolen logs from the Moosetowners.

These river people share no more than a dozen names, but such labels are little more than confirmations of identity: no matter how far he may wander from his birthplace, the Moosetowner is difficult to mistake. He speaks a soft-drawled English language of another century, and uses a paddle and a setting pole as if they were congenital appendages.

If mood could be voiced, what one might hear in this isolated settlement would be the sound of defiance. The Moosetowner smiles, but his smile is ambiguous: it can be a signal of friendship or a warning to walk softly. He lives by contention and glories in it: his resolve is to be left alone to do as he pleases.

Such terms are unacceptable to the world around him. The Moosetowner as a residual species in the family of man is probably doomed—and in our time, if the Army Engineers have their way. If the Dickey-Lincoln dams are built, the Moosetowner and his way of life will disappear under sixty feet of water.

And that, as Wonderland's no-nonsense Alice might have said, will be the end of that.

There was glory in driving a river. . . .

The long-log drive called for the best of these men. Some were young, most were grizzled . . . they all looked rawhide tough.

. . . No longer does timber kite down a wild Maine river . . . nor will it ever again.

THROUGH A GLASS DARKLY

Maine people belong to a race of rememberers. They never tire of being reminded that *This was the way it was.* Though the tracks are rusted and overgrown with weeds, in retinal memory the night train still waits at the wayside station. The people of this outland are unready to let go a rich and cherished past.

The reasons for this reluctance are good and sufficient. For centuries, Maine has stood in the position of the outsider, a vantage ground that afforded a detached and contemplative view of the surrounding world. Understandably, Maine people have yet to be convinced that this new world offers something better than the old.

Change is a harsh fact of life. Longfellow mourned at the passing of the village smithy, to no avail. Thoreau was appalled at the sight of his Indian guide in white man's garb, but change would not accommodate to his ideas of propriety. Maine is changing and will continue to change despite the demurs of the reluctant. How and at what pace this region will change is the substantial question.

In projecting Maine's future it is tempting to consider the example of the Deep South, which has moved in giant steps into the American industrial age. The analogy fails to satisfy. The South, emerging from slavery and a ruinous war, was shocked by the realization that its aristocratic agrarian culture was obsolete and gone with the wind. The only road open, if power and pride were to be regained, was industrialization. Maine's democratic dirt-farmer society, self-reliant by necessity, was unready and unwilling to meet the terms the new urban-based, growth-directed economy exacted.

Maine lost much of its small-town textile industry to the bustling South. Missing the boat was not a cause for rejoicing. Who then had the vision to see a blessing in the lost opportunity? Fatefully, the state missed the full brunt of the transmogrifying industrial convulsion which has scarred much of the nation and doomed the grassroots democracy that once characterized the American frontier. Gone are the plantation homes; disappearing are the open prairies, the small family spreads of the West and Middle West.

Essentially, the Industrial Revolution drove the people from the land and forced them into urban centers. The political power shifted from the small towns to the cities and city-based corporate conglomerates. Corporate philosophy became government philosophy, for the growing cities required food and energy that small patches of land and small units could not provide. The new economists proclaimed that only by continued booming growth could the American standard of living be sustained and poverty reduced. The Gross National Product became Holy Writ, and industrial gluttony was sanctified as The American Way.

In the process of stimulated growth, the people who lived on and by the land were largely forgotten. The provincialism that had thrived when America was a nation of small villages withered away. Today, only in northern New England have some vestiges of an earlier America survived.

Left in full and sole possession of a nineteenth-century world, the people of Maine have made the most of it. Rather than bemoaning the fate of being left behind, they have sedulously worked to furbish their singular image. Outlanders, increasingly weary of today and yearning for America's yesterdays, have been all too eager to collaborate in the effort. Maine is America's childhood, and childhood memories are dear.

Not that this Maine Mystique is totally synthetic. Maine is indeed the "outback" of the nation. Its citizens most certainly are distinguishable from the American prototype; and though the popular conception of the region as a place filled with moose, bear and crackerbox philosophers is hardly valid, rural wisdom remains a ruling force, and an occasional moose does wander down the main streets of its cities. The danger lies in embracing the image as a solution to the state's present and future problems.

It can be argued that the Maine Mystique may be more valuable than any new industry. Not long ago, when an oil refinery at Searsport was in prospect, the state's Environmental Protection Commission received a flood of protesting letters from all over the nation, and the majority of the writers had never so much as visited Maine. Since Maine does not have the resources to support the conventional idea of affluent life, it behooves the state to protect what it does possess—natural beauty and its special image. As L. L. Bean, an establishment which shrewdly exploits this image, has discovered, you can sell a shirt anywhere in the United States if you call it a Maine Guide Shirt.

The possession of this magical quality is all well and good, but what is becoming more and more apparent is that reliance upon this Valhalla image is compounding Maine's problems rather than curing them. What the state does not need in this time of transition is to be pictured as a paradise, or its natives to be cast in the role of folk heroes. Already such romanticizing has encouraged the notion that Maine is the last escape hatch for the disenchanted survivors of the failed American Dream.

The tragic irony is that the less significant the hard-scrabble farm has become as an economic factor, the more romantically is the rural life portrayed. And as less and less open countryside is available, the more alluring it becomes to the denizens of the crowded cities.

The state, commodious as it is, cannot serve as a lifeboat for the hordes seeking peace and personal salvation without sinking the lifeboat and destroying the very qualities that make it special. Nor can the state accede to the increasing pressures to open wide its doors to industrial development. The Far West is being called upon today to sacrifice its public lands and precious water in the hope that its coal and shale oil will help to balance the nation's energy budget. How Maine parries such pressures may well determine the state's future.

In the course of the past decade, rural Maine has attracted wave upon wave of homesteaders, retirees and counterculture drifters, many of the latter as ill-fitted to survive in this austere clime as the Pilgrim Fathers. The communes that enjoyed a brief flowering have for the most part disbanded, the survivors integrating with the social fabric of the villages as craftsmen, artists and jacks-of-all-trades, and contributing to the establishment of the consumer co-op movement, now a considerable factor in the Maine economy.

Perhaps more significant in terms of numbers and impact is the invasion of a young middle class. Disenchanted with the American success story, they come seeking sounder values for themselves and their growing children. Starved for the patina of antiquity, they restore crumbling early eighteenth-century homes with meticulous concern for authenticity. Community-minded, they are becoming part of village life and contributing skills, venture capital and a fresh vitality, assets offset to some degree by demands for better schools, services and certain ''frills'' that the early stock through the centuries of austerity had learned to live without.

This changing face of Maine has brought new problems, complexities that cannot be resolved with conventional political weapons. The local town meetings cannot rescind the basic law of supply and demand. The increasing demand for land has swollen land values, which in turn has attracted speculators who grow fat on a rising market. Developers whose love is not for the land but for the dollar are offering landed natives prices for land they cannot afford to refuse and are carving up open spaces to satisfy a market they themselves are stimulating with glowing pro-motionals. Retirees and summer sojourners are further inflating land values and in consequence raising real estate taxes to levels the low- and middle-income locals are finding increasingly burdensome.

It is in this climate of frustration that the new populism is finding its voice in Maine. We sometimes forget that American Democracy was a rural idea nurtured by Jefferson and reaffirmed by Jackson. The American Dream was shattered by the most violent technological explosion in the history of man. America became the most powerful nation in the world. The price it paid for the achievement of material wealth was a loss of sensibility, an atrophication of a sense of personal responsibility.

Maine has persisted as a culture of small villages, a society characterized by identity with place and strong tribal feelings of kinship for its own and with the land. Although the small working farm is no longer an important factor in the state's economy, Maine has remained essentially agrarian in spirit.

Today, Maine villages are demanding to be heard and to have a part in the decisions which affect their lives. In many cases, old-stock villagers have joined with ecology-minded newcomers on environmental issues, an uneasy alliance in view of the natives' deep-seated suspicion that the johnny-come-latelys hope to buy their way into heaven. Just as strange bedfellows are the fishermen and the well-to-do Keep Oil Out forces. The fishermen see heavy industry on the coast as a threat to their livelihood, while the affluent view the relatively unspoiled coast as one of the last sanctuaries for the privileged.

Whatever the constitution of these aroused citizen blocs and whatever their mixed motives, grassroots resistance to smokestacks and bulldozers has made a holding action possible. It would appear that the villagers are not fooled by the specious argument that Big Oil, Big Industry and Big Power will bring to Maine jobs and a higher standard of living. They suspect that the corporate giants will lure jobseekers rather than jobs, and invite a boom-and-bust economy with attendant slums and swollen welfare rolls. The State of Maine, it would appear, is not about to be beguiled by the failed concept of bigness. The state's vision of its future is closer to Dogpatch, U.S.A., than to Bayonne, New Jersey.

Nor are the citizens of the villages responding to the bureaucratic exhortations to consolidate schools, hospitals and other services in the putative interest of efficiency and economy. The towns that moved grudgingly in the past decade toward consolidation are yet to be convinced that they have gained on either score. Certainly the resistance to further abdication of local sovereignty is stiffening. In addition, the villages are becoming less and less disposed to accept state or federal largesse in the form of matching subsidies that offer financial aid at the price of absentee control.

The people of the state see another threat developing, one even more frightening for the seeming lack of weaponry to combat it. Perhaps no other state in the Union finds so much of its land falling into the hands of nonresidents. The vast majority of the wild and recreational lands are owned by out-of-state corporations which feel little or no obligation to consider Maine's interests when making decisions. No longer is this unhappy situation accepted with equanimity.

Populism is not a new phenomenon in this corner of America. The Greenback Party flourished shortly after the Civil War, and grassroots rebellion has surfaced sporadically ever since. The resurgence of the Democratic Party in the past several decades was clearly a reflection of frustration and a popular resentment against the special interests and the party in power which supported the narrow structure. Today, however, party labels are becoming less and less a voting consideration. Clearly, further decisions will be made not by political rhetoric but by issue-oriented independent voters genuinely concerned about the road ahead.

Maine at the crossroads sees its future through a glass darkly. What is clear is that the decisions made today will shape a course from which there is no return. On the side of optimism is the example of the Maine past. Always there has resided at the heart of the native consciousness the wisdom to know that those who own the land own the people, and only a people who own and honor its land can control its destiny.

And clearly too, Maine is saying something of value to America. Perhaps only those who live close to the soil can perceive the fallacies in the preachments of the economists who deal in figures rather than hearts and minds. At every hand, nature demonstrates that ecosystems support growth only to the point of equilibrium. There is a point where growth must slow, recycle, and failing that, collapse. Or as one philosopher put it, "The speed of a runaway horse is not important."

The shape of Maine's future turns upon how well its beleaguered villagers protect the land and order growth. In the meantime, the earth turns and the night train still waits at the wayside station.

Afterword

By Howard Chapnick
President, Black Star Publishing Company

God made the country, and Kosti Ruohomaa photographed it. For two decades this "Boswell of Maine characters" (as he was once described by a photography critic) lavished his love on the pastoral scene, the sea and the people who lived and worked close to nature.

Kosti was an artist. The word "art" is thrown around with gay abandon in photography—this picture looks like a Rembrandt, that one like a Renoir. That may be, but Kosti's photographs do not have to be compared to the work of painters. A Ruohomaa picture looks like a Ruohomaa!

He thought of himself as a Mencken-like cynic. He feared and hated the world of soapsuds, perfumed lipstick and conformity. I think that was why he photographed the rugged Yankee individualists, for, despite the fact that his thinking had moved far beyond their insularity, they at least fought with a passion for their views.

Kosti leaves a legacy of pictures. Some will be remembered for many years to come. But, more important, though he worked for money, he never let his ideas be beaten down.

I still recall his printing instructions on a contact sheet of a cemetery photograph that he wanted to be printed somberly dark. "It's gotta say," said Kosti, "YOU'RE GODDAM DEAD!"

I guess Kosti is "goddam dead," but the work he leaves behind him is "goddam" live.

The earth turns . . . and the night train still waits at the wayside station.